CONTENTS

SPANISH RICE

Servings: 4 - Prep: 10m - Cooks: 30m - Total: 40m

NUTRITION FACTS

Calories: 270, Carbohydrates: 45.7g, Fat: 7.6g, Protein: 4.8g, Cholesterol: 0mg

INGREDIENTS

- 2 tablespoons vegetable oil
- 2 cups water
- 1 cup uncooked white rice
- 1 (10 ounce) can diced tomatoes and green chiles
- 1 onion, chopped
- 2 teaspoons chili powder, or to taste
- ½ green bell pepper, chopped
- 1 teaspoon salt

DIRECTIONS

1. Heat oil in a deep skillet over medium heat. Saute rice, onion, and bell pepper until rice is browned and onions are tender.
2. Stir in water and tomatoes. Season with chili powder and salt. Cover, and simmer for 30 minutes, or until rice is cooked and liquid is absorbed.

OVEN ROASTED POTATOES

Servings: 4 - Prep: 15m - Cooks: 30m - Total: 45m

NUTRITION FACTS

Calories: 289, Carbohydrates: 53.1g, Fat: 7.1g, Protein: 5g, Cholesterol: 0mg

INGREDIENTS

- 1/8 cup olive oil
- ½ teaspoon dried oregano
- 1 tablespoon minced garlic
- ½ teaspoon dried parsley
- ½ teaspoon dried basil
- ½ teaspoon crushed red pepper flakes
- ½ teaspoon dried marjoram
- ½ teaspoon salt
- ½ teaspoon dried dill weed
- 4 large potatoes, peeled and cubed
- ½ teaspoon dried thyme

DIRECTIONS

1. Preheat oven to 475 degrees F (245 degrees C).
2. In a large bowl, combine oil, garlic, basil, marjoram, dill weed, thyme, oregano, parsley, red pepper flakes, and salt. Stir in potatoes until evenly coated. Place potatoes in a single layer on a roasting pan or baking sheet.
3. Roast for 20 to 30 minutes in the preheated oven, turning occasionally to brown on all sides.

PRETZEL TURTLES

Servings: 20 - Prep: 10m - Cooks: 4m - Total: 14m

NUTRITION FACTS

Calories: 82, Carbohydrates: 14.1g, Fat: 2.2g, Protein: 1.7g, Cholesterol: 1mg

INGREDIENTS

- 20 small mini pretzels
- 20 pecan halves
- 20 chocolate covered caramel candies

DIRECTIONS

1. Preheat oven to 300 degrees F (150 degrees C).
2. Arrange the pretzels in a single layer on a parchment lined cookie sheet. Place one chocolate covered caramel candy on each pretzel.
3. Bake for 4 minutes. While the candy is warm, press a pecan half onto each candy covered pretzel. Cool completely before storing in an airtight container.

FRIED RICE RESTAURANT STYLE

Servings: 8 - Prep: 15m - Cooks: 30m - Total: 45m

NUTRITION FACTS

Calories: 261, Carbohydrates: 39.7g, Fat: 8.4g, Protein: 5.8g, Cholesterol: 46mg

INGREDIENTS

- 2 cups enriched white rice
- 2 tablespoons vegetable oil
- 4 cups water
- 2 eggs
- 2/3 cup chopped baby carrots
- soy sauce to taste
- ½ cup frozen green peas
- sesame oil, to taste (optional)

DIRECTIONS

1. In a saucepan, combine rice and water. Bring to a boil. Reduce heat, cover, and simmer for 20 minutes.
2. In a small saucepan, boil carrots in water about 3 to 5 minutes. Drop peas into boiling water, and drain.
3. Heat wok over high heat. Pour in oil, then stir in carrots and peas; cook about 30 seconds. Crack in eggs, stirring quickly to scramble eggs with vegetables. Stir in cooked rice. Shake in soy sauce, and toss rice to coat. Drizzle with sesame oil, and toss again.

DUMPLINGS

Servings: 6 - Prep: 5m - Cooks: 15m - Total: 20m

NUTRITION FACTS

Calories: 105, Carbohydrates: 18g, Fat: 2.4g, Protein: 2.8g, Cholesterol: 2mg

INGREDIENTS

- 1 cup all-purpose flour
- ½ teaspoon salt
- 2 teaspoons baking powder
- 1 tablespoon margarine
- 1 teaspoon white sugar
- ½ cup milk

DIRECTIONS

1. Stir together flour, baking powder, sugar, and salt in medium size bowl. Cut in butter until crumbly. Stir in milk to make a soft dough.
2. Drop by spoonfuls into boiling stew. Cover and simmer 15 minutes without lifting lid. Serve.
3. To make parsley dumplings, add 1 tablespoon parsley flakes to the dry ingredients.

RED LENTIL CURRY

Servings: 8 - Prep: 10m - Cooks: 30m - Total: 40m

NUTRITION FACTS

Calories: 192, Carbohydrates: 32.5g, Fat: 2.6g, Protein: 12.1g, Cholesterol: 0mg

INGREDIENTS

- 2 cups red lentils
- 1 teaspoon chili powder
- 1 large onion, diced
- 1 teaspoon salt
- 1 tablespoon vegetable oil
- 1 teaspoon white sugar
- 2 tablespoons curry paste
- 1 teaspoon minced garlic
- 1 tablespoon curry powder

- 1 teaspoon minced fresh ginger
- 1 teaspoon ground turmeric
- 1 (14.25 ounce) can tomato puree
- 1 teaspoon ground cumin

DIRECTIONS

1. Wash the lentils in cold water until the water runs clear. Put lentils in a pot with enough water to cover; bring to a boil, place a cover on the pot, reduce heat to medium-low, and simmer, adding water during cooking as needed to keep covered, until tender, 15 to 20 minutes. Drain.
2. Heat vegetable oil in a large skillet over medium heat; cook and stir onions in hot oil until caramelized, about 20 minutes.
3. Mix curry paste, curry powder, turmeric, cumin, chili powder, salt, sugar, garlic, and ginger together in a large bowl; stir into the onions. Increase heat to high and cook, stirring constantly, until fragrant, 1 to 2 minutes.
4. Stir in the tomato puree, remove from heat and stir into the lentils.

BOSTON BAKED BEANS

Servings: 6 - Prep: 30m - Cooks: 4h - Total: 5h - Additional: 30m

NUTRITION FACTS

Calories: 382, Carbohydrates: 63.1g, Fat: 6.3g, Protein: 20.7g, Cholesterol: 14mg

INGREDIENTS

- 2 cups navy beans
- 1/4 teaspoon ground black pepper
- ½ pound bacon
- 1/4 teaspoon dry mustard
- 1 onion, finely diced
- ½ cup ketchup
- 3 tablespoons molasses
- 1 tablespoon Worcestershire sauce
- 2 teaspoons salt
- 1/4 cup brown sugar

DIRECTIONS

1. Soak beans overnight in cold water. Simmer the beans in the same water until tender, approximately 1 to 2 hours. Drain and reserve the liquid.
2. Preheat oven to 325 degrees F (165 degrees C).
3. Arrange the beans in a 2 quart bean pot or casserole dish by placing a portion of the beans in the bottom of dish, and layering them with bacon and onion.

4. In a saucepan, combine molasses, salt, pepper, dry mustard, ketchup, Worcestershire sauce and brown sugar. Bring the mixture to a boil and pour over beans. Pour in just enough of the reserved bean water to cover the beans. Cover the dish with a lid or aluminum foil.

5. Bake for 3 to 4 hours in the preheated oven, until beans are tender. Remove the lid about halfway through cooking, and add more liquid if necessary to prevent the beans from getting too dry.

BLACK BEANS AND RICE

Servings: 10 - Prep: 5m - Cooks: 25m - Total: 30m

NUTRITION FACTS

Calories: 140, Carbohydrates: 27.1g, Fat: 0.9g, Protein: 6.3g, Cholesterol: 0mg

INGREDIENTS

- 1 teaspoon olive oil
- 1 ½ cups low sodium, low fat vegetable broth
- 1 onion, chopped
- 1 teaspoon ground cumin
- 2 cloves garlic, minced
- 1/4 teaspoon cayenne pepper
- 3⁄4cup uncooked white rice
- 3 ½ cups canned black beans, drained

DIRECTIONS

1. In a stockpot over medium-high heat, heat the oil. Add the onion and garlic and saute for 4 minutes. Add the rice and saute for 2 minutes.

2. Add the vegetable broth, bring to a boil, cover and lower the heat and cook for 20 minutes. Add the spices and black beans.

MEXICAN RICE

Servings: 6 - Prep: 5m - Cooks: 25m - Total: 30m

NUTRITION FACTS

Calories: 158, Carbohydrates: 29.1g, Fat: 2.8g, Protein: 3.4g, Cholesterol: 1mg

INGREDIENTS

- 1 cup long grain white rice
- 1 tomato, seeded and chopped
- 1 tablespoon vegetable oil
- 1 cube chicken bouillon
- 1 ½ cups chicken broth
- salt and pepper to taste

- ½ onion, finely chopped
- ½ teaspoon ground cumin
- ½ green bell pepper, finely chopped
- ½ cup chopped fresh cilantro
- 1 fresh jalapeno pepper, chopped
- 1 clove garlic, halved

DIRECTIONS

1. In a medium sauce pan, cook rice in oil over medium heat for about 3 minutes. Pour in chicken broth, and bring to a boil. Stir in onion, green pepper, jalapeno, and diced tomato. Season with bouillon cube, salt and pepper, cumin, cilantro, and garlic. Bring to a boil, cover, and reduce heat to low. Cook for 20 minutes.

BROCCOLI BEEF

Servings: 4 - Prep: 15m - Cooks: 15m - Total: 30m

NUTRITION FACTS

Calories: 178, Carbohydrates: 19g, Fat: 3.2g, Protein: 19.2g, Cholesterol: 39mg

INGREDIENTS

- 1/4 cup all-purpose flour
- 1 pound boneless round steak, cut into bite size pieces
- 1 (10.5 ounce) can beef broth
- 1/4 teaspoon chopped fresh ginger root
- 2 tablespoons white sugar
- 1 clove garlic, minced
- 2 tablespoons soy sauce
- 4 cups chopped fresh broccoli

DIRECTIONS

1. In a small bowl, combine flour, broth, sugar, and soy sauce. Stir until sugar and flour are dissolved.
2. In a large skillet or wok over high heat, cook and stir beef 2 to 4 minutes, or until browned. Stir in broth mixture, ginger, garlic, and broccoli. Bring to a boil, then reduce heat. Simmer 5 to 10 minutes, or until sauce thickens.

PESTO PASTA WITH CHICKEN

Servings: 8 - Prep: 10m - Cooks: 20m - Total: 30m

NUTRITION FACTS

Calories: 328, Carbohydrates: 43.3g, Fat: 10.1g, Protein: 17.4g, Cholesterol: 22mg

INGREDIENTS

- 1 (16 ounce) package bow tie pasta
- crushed red pepper flakes to taste
- 1 teaspoon olive oil
- 1/3 cup oil-packed sun-dried tomatoes, drained and cut into strips
- 2 cloves garlic, minced
- ½ cup pesto sauce
- 2 boneless skinless chicken breasts, cut into bite-size pieces

DIRECTIONS

1. Bring a large pot of lightly salted water to a boil. Add pasta and cook for 8 to 10 minutes or until al dente; drain.
2. Heat oil in a large skillet over medium heat. Saute garlic until tender, then stir in chicken. Season with red pepper flakes. Cook until chicken is golden, and cooked through.
3. In a large bowl, combine pasta, chicken, sun-dried tomatoes and pesto. Toss to coat evenly.

ROASTED BEETS 'N' SWEETS

Servings: 6 - Prep: 15m - Cooks: 1h - Total: 1h15m

NUTRITION FACTS

Calories: 198, Carbohydrates: 34.3g, Fat: 5.9g, Protein: 3.5g, Cholesterol: 0mg

INGREDIENTS

- 6 medium beets, peeled and cut into chunks
- 1 teaspoon ground black pepper
- 2 ½ tablespoons olive oil, divided
- 1 teaspoon sugar
- 1 teaspoon garlic powder
- 3 medium sweet potatoes, cut into chunks
- 1 teaspoon kosher salt
- 1 large sweet onion, chopped

DIRECTIONS

1. Preheat oven to 400 degrees F (200 degrees C).
2. In a bowl, toss the beets with ½ tablespoon olive oil to coat. Spread in a single layer on a baking sheet.
3. Mix the remaining 2 tablespoons olive oil, garlic powder, salt, pepper, and sugar in a large resealable plastic bag. Place the sweet potatoes and onion in the bag. Seal bag, and shake to coat vegetables with the oil mixture.
4. Bake beets 15 minutes in the preheated oven. Mix sweet potato mixture with the beets on the baking sheet. Continue baking 45 minutes, stirring after 20 minutes, until all vegetables are tender.

SPICED SWEET ROASTED RED PEPPER HUMMUS

Servings: 8 - Prep: 15m - Cooks: 1h - Total: 1h15m - Additional: 1h

NUTRITION FACTS

Calories: 64, Carbohydrates: 9.6g, Fat: 2.2g, Protein: 2.5g, Cholesterol: 0mg

INGREDIENTS

- 1 (15 ounce) can garbanzo beans, drained
- ½ teaspoon ground cumin
- 1 (4 ounce) jar roasted red peppers
- ½ teaspoon cayenne pepper
- 3 tablespoons lemon juice
- 1/4 teaspoon salt
- 1 ½ tablespoons tahini
- 1 tablespoon chopped fresh parsley
- 1 clove garlic, minced

DIRECTIONS

1. In an electric blender or food processor, puree the chickpeas, red peppers, lemon juice, tahini, garlic, cumin, cayenne, and salt. Process, using long pulses, until the mixture is fairly smooth, and slightly fluffy. Make sure to scrape the mixture off the sides of the food processor or blender in between pulses. Transfer to a serving bowl and refrigerate for at least 1 hour. (The hummus can be made up to 3 days ahead and refrigerated. Return to room temperature before serving.)
2. Sprinkle the hummus with the chopped parsley before serving.

BAKED SWEET POTATOES

Servings: 4 - Prep: 10m - Cooks: 1h5m - Total: 1h15m

NUTRITION FACTS

Calories: 321, Carbohydrates: 61g, Fat: 7.3g, Protein: 4.8g, Cholesterol: 0mg

INGREDIENTS

- 2 tablespoons olive oil
- 2 pinches salt
- 3 large sweet potatoes
- 2 pinches ground black pepper
- 2 pinches dried oregano

DIRECTIONS

1. Preheat oven to 350 degrees F (175 degrees C). Coat the bottom of a glass or non-stick baking dish with olive oil, just enough to coat.
2. Wash and peel the sweet potatoes. Cut them into medium size pieces. Place the cut sweet potatoes in the baking dish and turn them so that they are coated with the olive oil. Sprinkle moderately with oregano, and salt and pepper (to taste).
3. Bake in a preheated 350 degrees F (175 degrees C) oven for 60 minutes or until soft.

VIETNAMESE FRESH SPRING ROLLS

Servings: 8 - Prep: 45m - Cooks: 5m - Total: 50m

NUTRITION FACTS

Calories: 82, Carbohydrates: 15.8g, Fat: 0.7g, Protein: 3.3g, Cholesterol: 11mg

INGREDIENTS

- 2 ounces rice vermicelli
- 1/4 cup water
- 8 rice wrappers (8.5 inch diameter)
- 2 tablespoons fresh lime juice
- 8 large cooked shrimp - peeled, deveined and cut in half
- 1 clove garlic, minced
- 1 1/3 tablespoons chopped fresh Thai basil
- 2 tablespoons white sugar
- 3 tablespoons chopped fresh mint leaves
- ½ teaspoon garlic chili sauce
- 3 tablespoons chopped fresh cilantro
- 3 tablespoons hoisin sauce
- 2 leaves lettuce, chopped
- 1 teaspoon finely chopped peanuts
- 4 teaspoons fish sauce

DIRECTIONS

1. Bring a medium saucepan of water to boil. Boil rice vermicelli 3 to 5 minutes, or until al dente, and drain.
2. Fill a large bowl with warm water. Dip one wrapper into the hot water for 1 second to soften. Lay wrapper flat. In a row across the center, place 2 shrimp halves, a handful of vermicelli, basil, mint, cilantro and lettuce, leaving about 2 inches uncovered on each side. Fold uncovered sides inward, then tightly roll the wrapper, beginning at the end with the lettuce. Repeat with remaining ingredients.
3. In a small bowl, mix the fish sauce, water, lime juice, garlic, sugar and chili sauce.
4. In another small bowl, mix the hoisin sauce and peanuts.
5. Serve rolled spring rolls with the fish sauce and hoisin sauce mixtures.

CHICKPEA CURRY

Servings: 8 - Prep: 10m - Cooks: 30m - Total: 40m

NUTRITION FACTS

Calories: 135, Carbohydrates: 20.5g, Fat: 4.5g, Protein: 4.1g, Cholesterol: 0mg

INGREDIENTS

- 2 tablespoons vegetable oil
- 1 teaspoon ground coriander
- 2 onions, minced
- salt
- 2 cloves garlic, minced
- 1 teaspoon cayenne pepper
- 2 teaspoons fresh ginger root, finely chopped
- 1 teaspoon ground turmeric
- 6 whole cloves
- 2 (15 ounce) cans garbanzo beans
- 2 (2 inch) sticks cinnamon, crushed
- 1 cup chopped fresh cilantro
- 1 teaspoon ground cumin

DIRECTIONS

1. Heat oil in a large frying pan over medium heat, and fry onions until tender.
2. Stir in garlic, ginger, cloves, cinnamon, cumin, coriander, salt, cayenne, and turmeric. Cook for 1 minute over medium heat, stirring constantly. Mix in garbanzo beans and their liquid. Continue to cook and stir until all ingredients are well blended and heated through. Remove from heat. Stir in cilantro just before serving, reserving 1 tablespoon for garnish.

ROAST POTATOES

Servings: 4 - Prep: 10m - Cooks: 20m - Total: 30m

NUTRITION FACTS

Calories: 227, Carbohydrates: 36.4g, Fat: 7.3g, Protein: 4.3g, Cholesterol: 0mg

INGREDIENTS

- 2 pounds red potatoes, cut into quarters
- ½ teaspoon freshly ground black pepper
- 2 tablespoons vegetable oil
- ½ teaspoon dried rosemary, crushed
- 1 teaspoon salt

DIRECTIONS

1. Preheat oven to 450 degrees F (250 degrees C).
2. Place potatoes in a large roasting pan and toss with oil, salt, pepper, and rosemary until evenly coated. Spread out potatoes in a single layer.
3. Bake in preheated oven for 20 minutes, stirring occasionally. Serve immediately.

BAKED BEANS

Servings: 6 - Prep: 20m - Cooks: 1h - Total: 1h20m

NUTRITION FACTS

Calories: 287, Carbohydrates: 52.3g, Fat: 6.5g, Protein: 8.9g, Cholesterol: 16mg

INGREDIENTS

- 2 (15 ounce) cans baked beans with pork
- 1 teaspoon Worcestershire sauce
- ½ cup packed brown sugar
- 1 teaspoon red wine vinegar
- ½ onion, chopped
- salt and pepper to taste
- ½ cup ketchup
- 2 slices bacon
- 1 tablespoon prepared mustard

DIRECTIONS

1. Preheat oven to 350 degrees F (175 degrees C).
2. In a 9x9 inch baking dish, combine the pork and beans, brown sugar, onion, ketchup, mustard, Worcestershire sauce and vinegar and season with salt and pepper to taste. Top with the bacon slices.
3. Bake at 350 degrees F (175 degrees C) for 1 hour, or until sauce is thickened and bacon is cooked.

THAI PEANUT CHICKEN

Servings: 8 - Prep: 25m - Cooks: 15m - Total: 40m

NUTRITION FACTS

Calories: 360, Carbohydrates: 43.4g, Fat: 11.3g, Protein: 21g, Cholesterol: 34mg

INGREDIENTS

- 2 cups uncooked white rice
- 4 skinless, boneless chicken breast halves - cut into thin strips
- 4 cups water
- 3 tablespoons chopped garlic
- 3 tablespoons soy sauce

- 1 ½ tablespoons chopped fresh ginger root
- 2 tablespoons creamy peanut butter
- ¾cup chopped green onions
- 2 teaspoons white wine vinegar
- 2 ½ cups broccoli florets
- 1/4 teaspoon cayenne pepper
- 1/3 cup unsalted dry-roasted peanuts
- 3 tablespoons olive oil

DIRECTIONS

1. Combine the rice and water in a saucepan over medium-high heat. Bring to a boil, then reduce heat to low, cover, and simmer for 20 minutes, or until rice is tender. In a small bowl, stir together the soy sauce, peanut butter, vinegar, and cayenne pepper. Set aside.
2. Heat oil in a skillet or wok over high heat. Add chicken, garlic and ginger, and cook, stirring constantly, until chicken is golden on the outside, about 5 minutes.
3. Reduce heat to medium, and add green onion, broccoli, peanuts, and the peanut butter mixture. Cook, stirring frequently, for 5 minutes, or until broccoli is tender, and chicken is cooked through. Serve over rice.

SPICY BAKED SWEET POTATO FRIES

Servings: 6 - Prep: 10m - Cooks: 1h - Total: 1h10m

NUTRITION FACTS

Calories: 169, Carbohydrates: 29.2g, Fat: 4.7g, Protein: 2.1g, Cholesterol: 0mg

INGREDIENTS

- 6 sweet potatoes, cut into French fries
- 3 tablespoons taco seasoning mix
- 2 tablespoons canola oil
- 1/4 teaspoon cayenne pepper

DIRECTIONS

1. Preheat the oven to 425 degrees F (220 degrees C).
2. In a plastic bag, combine the sweet potatoes, canola oil, taco seasoning, and cayenne pepper. Close and shake the bag until the fries are evenly coated. Spread the fries out in a single layer on two large baking sheets.
3. Bake for 30 minutes, or until crispy and brown on one side. Turn the fries over using a spatula, and cook for another 30 minutes, or until they are all crispy on the outside and tender inside. Thinner fries may not take as long.

BUFFALO CHICKEN FINGERS

Servings: 8 - Prep: 20m - Cooks: 20m - Total: 40m

NUTRITION FACTS

Calories: 125, Carbohydrates: 10.7g, Fat: 2g, Protein: 15g, Cholesterol: 34mg

INGREDIENTS

- 4 skinless, boneless chicken breast halves - cut into finger-sized pieces
- ½ teaspoon salt
- 1/4 cup all-purpose flour
- 3⁄4cup bread crumbs
- 1 teaspoon garlic powder
- 2 egg whites, beaten
- 1 teaspoon cayenne pepper
- 1 tablespoon water

DIRECTIONS

1. Preheat oven to 400 degrees F (205 degrees C). Coat a baking sheet with a nonstick spray.
2. In a bag, mix together flour, ½ teaspoon garlic powder, ½ teaspoon cayenne pepper, and 1/4 teaspoon salt. On a plate, mix the bread crumbs with the rest of the garlic powder, cayenne pepper, and salt.
3. Shake the chicken pieces with the seasoned flour. Beat egg whites with 1 tablespoon water, and place egg mixture in a shallow dish or bowl. Dip seasoned chicken in egg mixture, then roll in the seasoned bread crumb mixture. Place on prepared baking sheet.
4. Bake for about 8 minutes in the preheated oven. Use tongs to turn pieces over. Bake 8 minutes longer, or until chicken juices run clear.

MUSHROOM RICE

Servings: 4 - Prep: 5m - Cooks: 25m - Total: 30m

NUTRITION FACTS

Calories: 216, Carbohydrates: 41.1g, Fat: 2.8g, Protein: 5.3g, Cholesterol: 8mg

INGREDIENTS

- 2 teaspoons butter
- 2 cups chicken broth
- 6 mushrooms, coarsely chopped
- 1 cup uncooked white rice
- 1 clove garlic, minced
- ½ teaspoon chopped fresh parsley
- 1 green onion, finely chopped
- salt and pepper to taste

DIRECTIONS

1. Melt butter in a saucepan over medium heat. Cook mushrooms, garlic and green onion until mushrooms are cooked and liquid has evaporated. Stir in chicken broth and rice. Season with parsley, salt and pepper. Reduce heat, cover and simmer for 20 minutes.

COD WITH ITALIAN CRUMB TOPPING

Servings: 4 - Prep: 15m - Cooks: 10m - Total: 25m

NUTRITION FACTS

Calories: 131, Carbohydrates: 7g, Fat: 2.9g, Protein: 18.1g, Cholesterol: 39mg

INGREDIENTS

- 1/4 cup fine dry bread crumbs
- 1/8 teaspoon garlic powder
- 2 tablespoons grated Parmesan cheese
- 1/8 teaspoon ground black pepper
- 1 tablespoon cornmeal
- 4 (3 ounce) fillets cod fillets
- 1 teaspoon olive oil
- 1 egg white, lightly beaten
- ½ teaspoon Italian seasoning

DIRECTIONS

1. Preheat oven to 450 degrees F (230 degrees C).
2. In a small shallow bowl, stir together the bread crumbs, cheese, cornmeal, oil, italian seasoning, garlic powder and pepper; set aside.
3. Coat the rack of a broiling pan with cooking spray. Place the cod on the rack, folding under any thin edges of the filets. Brush with the egg white, then spoon the crumb mixture evenly on top.
4. Bake in a preheated oven for 10 to 12 minutes or until the fish flakes easily when tested with a fork and is opaque all the way through.

TOMATILLO SALSA VERDE

Servings: 8 - Prep: 10m - Cooks: 15m - Total: 25m

NUTRITION FACTS

Calories: 24, Carbohydrates: 4.6g, Fat: 0.6g, Protein: 0.8g, Cholesterol: 0mg

INGREDIENTS

- 1 pound tomatillos, husked
- 1 tablespoon chopped fresh oregano
- ½ cup finely chopped onion

- ½ teaspoon ground cumin
- 1 teaspoon minced garlic
- 1 ½ teaspoons salt, or to taste
- 1 serrano chile peppers, minced
- 2 cups water
- 2 tablespoons chopped cilantro

DIRECTIONS

1. Place tomatillos, onion, garlic, and chile pepper into a saucepan. Season with cilantro, oregano, cumin, and salt; pour in water. Bring to a boil over high heat, then reduce heat to medium-low, and simmer until the tomatillos are soft, 10 to 15 minutes.
2. Using a blender, carefully puree the tomatillos and water in batches until smooth.

GREEK PASTA WITH TOMATOES AND WHITE BEANS

Servings: 4 - Prep: 10m - Cooks: 15m - Total: 25m

NUTRITION FACTS

Calories: 460, Carbohydrates: 79g, Fat: 5.9g, Protein: 23.4g, Cholesterol: 17mg

INGREDIENTS

- 2 (14.5 ounce) cans Italian-style diced tomatoes
- 8 ounces penne pasta
- 1 (19 ounce) can cannellini beans, drained and rinsed
- ½ cup crumbled feta cheese
- 10 ounces fresh spinach, washed and chopped

DIRECTIONS

1. Cook the pasta in a large pot of boiling salted water until al dente.
2. Meanwhile, combine tomatoes and beans in a large non-stick skillet. Bring to a boil over medium high heat. Reduce heat, and simmer 10 minutes.
3. Add spinach to the sauce; cook for 2 minutes or until spinach wilts, stirring constantly.
4. Serve sauce over pasta, and sprinkle with feta.

AMATRICIANA

Servings: 4 - Prep: 15m - Cooks: 20m - Total: 35m

NUTRITION FACTS

Calories: 529, Carbohydrates: 97.6g, Fat: 7.5g, Protein: 21.5g, Cholesterol: 12mg

INGREDIENTS

- 4 slices bacon, diced
- 2 (14.5 ounce) cans stewed tomatoes
- ½ cup chopped onion
- 1 pound linguine pasta, uncooked
- 1 teaspoon minced garlic
- 1 tablespoon chopped fresh basil
- 1/4 teaspoon crushed red pepper flakes
- 2 tablespoons grated Parmesan cheese

DIRECTIONS

1. Cook diced bacon in a large saucepan over medium high heat until crisp, about 5 minutes. Drain all but 2 tablespoons of drippings from the pan.
2. Add onions, and cook over medium heat about 3 minutes. Stir in garlic and red pepper flakes; cook 30 seconds. Add canned tomatoes, undrained; simmer 10 minutes, breaking up tomatoes.
3. Meanwhile, cook the pasta in a large pot of 4 quarts boiling salted water until al dente. Drain.
4. Stir basil into the sauce, and then toss with cooked pasta. Serve with grated Parmesan cheese.

EASY RED BEANS AND RICE

Servings: 8 - Prep: 10m - Cooks: 30m - Total: 40m

NUTRITION FACTS

Calories: 289, Carbohydrates: 42.4g, Fat: 5.7g, Protein: 16.3g, Cholesterol: 35mg

INGREDIENTS

- 2 cups water
- 2 (15 ounce) cans canned kidney beans, drained
- 1 cup uncooked rice
- 1 (16 ounce) can whole peeled tomatoes, chopped
- 1 (16 ounce) package turkey kielbasa, cut diagonally into 1/4 inch slices
- ½ teaspoon dried oregano
- 1 onion, chopped
- salt to taste
- 1 green bell pepper, chopped
- ½ teaspoon pepper
- 1 clove chopped garlic

DIRECTIONS

1. In a saucepan, bring water to a boil. Add rice and stir. Reduce heat, cover and simmer for 20 minutes.
2. In a large skillet over low heat, cook sausage for 5 minutes. Stir in onion, green pepper and garlic; saute until tender. Pour in beans and tomatoes with juice. Season with oregano, salt and pepper. Simmer uncovered for 20 minutes. Serve over rice.

PICO DE GALLO

Servings: 12 - Prep: 20m - Cooks: 3h - Total: 3h20m - Additional: 3h

NUTRITION FACTS

Calories: 10, Carbohydrates: 2.2g, Fat: 0.1g, Protein: 0.4g, Cholesterol: 0mg

INGREDIENTS

- 6 roma (plum) tomatoes, diced
- 1 clove garlic, minced
- ½ red onion, minced
- 1 pinch garlic powder
- 3 tablespoons chopped fresh cilantro
- 1 pinch ground cumin, or to taste
- ½ jalapeno pepper, seeded and minced
- salt and ground black pepper to taste
- ½ lime, juiced

DIRECTIONS

1. Stir the tomatoes, onion, cilantro, jalapeno pepper, lime juice, garlic, garlic powder, cumin, salt, and pepper together in a bowl. Refrigerate at least 3 hours before serving.

PASTA WITH SCALLOPS, ZUCCHINI, AND TOMATOES

Servings: 8 - Prep: 15m - Cooks: 15m - Total: 30m

NUTRITION FACTS

Calories: 335, Carbohydrates: 46.1g, Fat: 9.1g, Protein: 18.7g, Cholesterol: 20mg

INGREDIENTS

- 1 pound dry fettuccine pasta
- ½ teaspoon crushed red pepper flakes
- 1/4 cup olive oil
- 1 cup chopped fresh basil
- 3 cloves garlic, minced
- 4 roma (plum) tomatoes, chopped
- 2 zucchinis, diced
- 1 pound bay scallops
- ½ teaspoon salt
- 2 tablespoons grated Parmesan cheese

DIRECTIONS

1. In a large pot with boiling salted water cook pasta until al dente. Drain.
2. Meanwhile, in a large skillet heat oil, add garlic and cook until tender. Add the zucchini, salt, red pepper flakes, dried basil (if using) and saute for 10 minutes. Add chopped tomatoes, bay scallops, and fresh basil (if using) and simmer for 5 minutes, or until scallops are opaque.
3. Pour sauce over cooked pasta and serve with grated Parmesan cheese.

ONE SKILLET MEXICAN QUINOA

Servings: 4 - Prep: 15m - Cooks: 25m - Total: 40m

NUTRITION FACTS

Calories: 450, Carbohydrates: 67.1g, Fat: 14.9g, Protein: 16.5g, Cholesterol: 2mg

INGREDIENTS

- 1 tablespoon olive oil
- 1 tablespoon red pepper flakes, or to taste
- 1 jalapeno pepper, chopped
- 1 ½ teaspoons chili powder
- 2 cloves garlic, chopped
- ½ teaspoon cumin
- 1 (15 ounce) can black beans, rinsed and drained
- 1 pinch kosher salt and ground black pepper to taste
- 1 (14.5 ounce) can fire-roasted diced tomatoes
- 1 avocado - peeled, pitted, and diced
- 1 cup yellow corn
- 1 lime, juiced
- 1 cup quinoa
- 2 tablespoons chopped fresh cilantro
- 1 cup chicken broth

DIRECTIONS

1. Heat oil in a large skillet over medium-high heat. Saute jalapeno pepper and garlic in hot oil until fragrant, about 1 minute.
2. Stir black beans, tomatoes, yellow corn, quinoa, and chicken broth into skillet; season with red pepper flakes, chili powder, cumin, salt, and black pepper. Bring to a boil, cover the skillet with a lid, reduce heat to low, and simmer until quinoa is tender and liquid is mostly absorbed, about 20 minutes. Stir avocado, lime juice, and cilantro into quinoa until combined.

CAJUN STYLE BAKED SWEET POTATO

Servings: 4 - Prep: 10m - Cooks: 1h - Total: 1h10m

Calories: 229, Carbohydrates: 49.1g, Fat: 2.3g, Protein: 4.8g, Cholesterol: 0mg

INGREDIENTS

- 1 ½ teaspoons paprika
- 1/4 teaspoon dried rosemary
- 1 teaspoon brown sugar
- 1/4 teaspoon garlic powder
- 1/4 teaspoon black pepper
- 1/8 teaspoon cayenne pepper
- 1/4 teaspoon onion powder
- 2 large sweet potatoes
- 1/4 teaspoon dried thyme
- 1 ½ teaspoons olive oil

DIRECTIONS

1. Preheat oven to 375 degrees F (190 degrees C).
2. In a small bowl, stir together paprika, brown sugar, black pepper, onion powder, thyme, rosemary, garlic powder, and cayenne pepper.
3. Slice the sweet potatoes in half lengthwise. Brush each half with olive oil. Rub the seasoning mix over the cut surface of each half. Place sweet potatoes on a baking sheet, or in a shallow pan.
4. Bake in preheated oven until tender, or about 1 hour.

SPICY PEACH-GLAZED PORK CHOPS

Servings: 4 - Prep: 10m - Cooks: 20m - Total: 30m

NUTRITION FACTS

Calories: 404, Carbohydrates: 58.2g, Fat: 11.5g, Protein: 13.2g, Cholesterol: 36mg

INGREDIENTS

- 1 cup peach preserves
- 1 pinch ground cinnamon
- 1 ½ tablespoons Worcestershire sauce
- salt and pepper to taste
- ½ teaspoon chile paste
- 2 tablespoons vegetable oil
- 4 boneless pork chops
- ½ cup white wine
- 1 teaspoon ground ginger

DIRECTIONS

1. In a small bowl, mix together the peach preserves, Worcestershire sauce, and chile paste. Rinse pork chops, and pat dry. Sprinkle the chops with ginger, cinnamon, salt, and pepper.
2. Heat oil in a large skillet over medium-high heat. Sear the chops for about 2 minutes on each side. Remove from the pan, and set aside.
3. Pour white wine into the pan, and stir to scrape the bottom of the pan. Stir in the peach preserves mixture. Return the chops to the pan, and flip to coat with the sauce. Reduce heat to medium low, and cook the pork chops for about 8 minutes on each side, or until done.

AUTHENTIC FRENCH MERINGUES

Servings: 36 - Prep: 20m - Cooks: 3h - Total: 3h20m

NUTRITION FACTS

Calories: 31, Carbohydrates: 7.5g, Fat: 0g, Protein: 0.4g, Cholesterol: 0mg

INGREDIENTS

- 4 egg whites
- 2 1/4 cups confectioners' sugar

DIRECTIONS

1. Preheat the oven to 200 degrees F (95 degrees C). Butter and flour a baking sheet.
2. In a glass or metal bowl, whip egg whites until foamy using an electric mixer. Sprinkle in sugar a little at a time, while continuing to whip at medium speed. When the mixture becomes stiff and shiny like satin, stop mixing, and transfer the mixture to a large pastry bag. Pipe the meringue out onto the prepared baking sheet using a large round tip or star tip.
3. Place the meringues in the oven and place a wooden spoon handle in the door to keep it from closing all the way. Bake for 3 hours, or until the meringues are dry, and can easily be removed from the pan. Allow cookies to cool completely before storing in an airtight container at room temperature.

BAKED FRENCH FRIES

Servings: 4 - Prep: 20m - Cooks: 25m - Total: 45m

NUTRITION FACTS

Calories: 145, Carbohydrates: 28.2g, Fat: 1.6g, Protein: 5.2g, Cholesterol: 4mg

INGREDIENTS

- 3 russet potatoes, sliced into 1/4 inch strips
- 1/4 cup grated Parmesan cheese
- cooking spray
- salt and pepper to taste
- 1 teaspoon dried basil

DIRECTIONS

1. Preheat oven to 400 degrees F (200 degrees C). Lightly grease a medium baking sheet.

2. Arrange potato strips in a single layer on the prepared baking sheet, skin sides down. Spray lightly with cooking spray, and sprinkle with basil, Parmesan cheese, salt and pepper.
3. Bake 25 minutes in the preheated oven, or until golden brown.

SUPERFAST ASPARAGUS

Servings: 3 - Prep: 5m - Cooks: 10m - Total: 15m

NUTRITION FACTS

Calories: 32, Carbohydrates: 6.3g, Fat: 0.2g, Protein: 3.4g, Cholesterol: 0mg

INGREDIENTS

- 1 pound asparagus
- 1 teaspoon Cajun seasoning

DIRECTIONS

1. Preheat oven to 425 degrees F (220 degrees C).
2. Snap the asparagus at the tender part of the stalk. Arrange spears in one layer on a baking sheet. Spray lightly with nonstick spray; sprinkle with the Cajun seasoning.
3. Bake in the preheated oven until tender, about 10 minutes.

OVEN ROASTED RED POTATOES AND ASPARAGUS

Servings: 6 - Prep: 15m - Cooks: 45m - Total: 1h

NUTRITION FACTS

Calories: 149, Carbohydrates: 23.5g, Fat: 4.9g, Protein: 4.2g, Cholesterol: 0mg

INGREDIENTS

- 1 ½ pounds red potatoes, cut into chunks
- 4 teaspoons dried thyme
- 2 tablespoons extra virgin olive oil
- 2 teaspoons kosher salt
- 8 cloves garlic, thinly sliced
- 1 bunch fresh asparagus, trimmed and cut into 1 inch pieces
- 4 teaspoons dried rosemary
- ground black pepper to taste

DIRECTIONS

1. Preheat oven to 425 degrees F (220 degrees C).
2. In a large baking dish, toss the red potatoes with ½ the olive oil, garlic, rosemary, thyme, and ½ the kosher salt. Cover with aluminum foil.

3. Bake 20 minutes in the preheated oven. Mix in the asparagus, remaining olive oil, and remaining salt. Cover, and continue cooking 15 minutes, or until the potatoes are tender. Increase oven temperature to 450 degrees F (230 degrees C). Remove foil, and continue cooking 5 to 10 minutes, until potatoes are lightly browned. Season with pepper to serve.

QUINOA WITH CHICKPEAS AND TOMATOES

Servings: 6 - Prep: 20m - Cooks: 20m - Total: 40m

NUTRITION FACTS

Calories: 185, Carbohydrates: 28.8g, Fat: 5.4g, Protein: 6g, Cholesterol: 0mg

INGREDIENTS

- 1 cup quinoa
- 3 tablespoons lime juice
- 1/8 teaspoon salt
- 4 teaspoons olive oil
- 1   3/4cups water
- ½ teaspoon ground cumin
- 1 cup canned garbanzo beans (chickpeas), drained
- 1 pinch salt and pepper to taste
- 1 tomato, chopped
- ½ teaspoon chopped fresh parsley
- 1 clove garlic, minced

DIRECTIONS

1. Place the quinoa in a fine mesh strainer, and rinse under cold, running water until the water no longer foams. Bring the quinoa, salt, and water to a boil in a saucepan. Reduce heat to medium-low, cover, and simmer until the quinoa is tender, 20 to 25 minutes.
2. Once done, stir in the garbanzo beans, tomatoes, garlic, lime juice, and olive oil. Season with cumin, salt, and pepper. Sprinkle with chopped fresh parsley to serve.

JAMIE'S SWEET AND EASY CORN ON THE COB

Servings: 6 - Prep: 5m - Cooks: 10m - Total: 15m

NUTRITION FACTS

Calories: 94, Carbohydrates: 21.5g, Fat: 1.1g, Protein: 2.9g, Cholesterol: 0mg

INGREDIENTS

- 2 tablespoons white sugar
- 6 ears corn on the cob, husks and silk removed
- 1 tablespoon lemon juice

DIRECTIONS

1. Fill a large pot about   3⁄4full of water and bring to a boil. Stir in sugar and lemon juice, dissolving the sugar. Gently place ears of corn into boiling water, cover the pot, turn off the heat, and let the corn cook in the hot water until tender, about 10 minutes.

ANGEL HAIR PASTA CHICKEN

Servings: 6 - Prep: 10m - Cooks: 20m - Total: 30m

NUTRITION FACTS

Calories: 282, Carbohydrates: 34.7g, Fat: 8.4g, Protein: 17.7g, Cholesterol: 28mg

INGREDIENTS

- 2 tablespoons olive oil, divided
- 2 cloves garlic, minced
- 2 skinless, boneless chicken breast halves - cubed
- 2/3 cup chicken broth
- 12 ounces angel hair pasta
- 1 teaspoon dried basil
- 1 carrot, sliced diagonally into 1/4 inch thick slices
- 1/4 cup grated Parmesan cheese
- 1 (10 ounce) package frozen broccoli florets, thawed

DIRECTIONS

1. Heat 1 tablespoon oil in a medium skillet over medium heat. Add chicken and saute for 5 to 7 minutes, or until chicken is cooked through (no longer pink). Remove from skillet and drain on paper towels.
2. Bring a large pot of lightly salted water to a boil. Add pasta and cook for 2 to 4 minutes, or until al dente; drain and set aside.
3. While pasta is cooking, heat 2nd tablespoon oil over medium heat in same skillet used for chicken. Stir fry carrots for about 4 minutes, then add broccoli and garlic and stir fry for another 2 minutes. Finally, stir in broth, basil and cheese and return chicken to skillet. Reduce heat to low and simmer for about 4 minutes.
4. Place drained pasta in a large serving bowl. Top with chicken/vegetable mixture and serve immediately.

INDIAN STYLE BASMATI RICE

Servings: 6 - Prep: 10m - Cooks: 25m - Total: 45m - Additional: 10m

NUTRITION FACTS

Calories: 216, Carbohydrates: 38.9g, Fat: 5.4g, Protein: 3.9g, Cholesterol: 0mg

INGREDIENTS

- 1 ½ cups basmati rice
- 1 tablespoon cumin seed
- 2 tablespoons vegetable oil
- 1 teaspoon salt, or to taste
- 1 (2 inch) piece cinnamon stick
- 2 ½ cups water
- 2 pods green cardamom
- 1 small onion, thinly sliced
- 2 whole cloves

DIRECTIONS

1. Place rice into a bowl with enough water to cover. Set aside to soak for 20 minutes.
2. Heat the oil in a large pot or saucepan over medium heat. Add the cinnamon stick, cardamom pods, cloves, and cumin seed. Cook and stir for about a minute, then add the onion to the pot. Saute the onion until a rich golden brown, about 10 minutes. Drain the water from the rice, and stir into the pot. Cook and stir the rice for a few minutes, until lightly toasted. Add salt and water to the pot, and bring to a boil. Cover, and reduce heat to low. Simmer for about 15 minutes, or until all of the water has been absorbed. Let stand for 5 minutes, then fluff with a fork before serving.

ALFREDO LIGHT

Servings: 8 - Prep: 20m - Cooks: 20m - Total: 40m

NUTRITION FACTS

Calories: 292, Carbohydrates: 50.5g, Fat: 4.1g, Protein: 13.9g, Cholesterol: 6mg

INGREDIENTS

- 1 onion, chopped
- ½ teaspoon salt
- 1 clove garlic, minced
- 1/4 teaspoon ground black pepper
- 2 teaspoons vegetable oil
- ½ cup grated Parmesan cheese
- 2 cups skim milk
- 16 ounces dry fettuccine pasta
- 1 cup chicken broth
- 1 (16 ounce) package frozen broccoli florets
- 3 tablespoons all-purpose flour

DIRECTIONS

1. In a medium saucepan, heat oil over medium heat. Add onion and garlic, and saute until golden brown.

2. In a small saucepan, stir together milk, chicken broth, flour, salt and pepper over low heat until smooth and thick. Stir into onion mixture. Continue to cook over medium low heat, stirring frequently, until the sauce is thick. Stir in Parmesan cheese.
3. Meanwhile, cook pasta in boiling water. Add broccoli to the pasta for the last several minutes of cooking. Continue cooking until the pasta is al dente.
4. Drain the pasta and vegetables, and transfer to a large bowl. Toss with sauce. Serve.

OVEN FRIES

Servings: 6 - Prep: 15m - Cooks: 30m - Total: 45m

NUTRITION FACTS

Calories: 156, Carbohydrates: 34.1g, Fat: 1g, Protein: 3.8g, Cholesterol: 0mg

INGREDIENTS

- 2 ½ pounds baking potatoes
- 1 teaspoon salt
- 1 teaspoon vegetable oil
- 1 pinch ground cayenne pepper
- 1 tablespoon white sugar

DIRECTIONS

1. Preheat oven to 450 degrees F (230 degrees C). Line a baking sheet with foil, and coat well with vegetable cooking spray. Scrub potatoes well and cut into ½ inch thick fries.
2. In a large mixing bowl, toss potatoes with oil, sugar, salt and red pepper. Spread on baking sheet in one layer.
3. Bake for 30 minutes in the preheated oven, until potatoes are tender and browned. Serve immediately.

SWEET AND SOUR SAUCE

Servings: 48 - Prep: 5m - Cooks: 15m - Total: 20m

NUTRITION FACTS

Calories: 32, Carbohydrates: 8.1g, Fat: 0g, Protein: 0.2g, Cholesterol: 0mg

INGREDIENTS

- 2 cups water
- 1 (6 ounce) can tomato paste
- 2/3 cup distilled white vinegar
- 1 (8 ounce) can pineapple tidbits, drained
- 1 ½ cups white sugar
- 3 tablespoons cornstarch

DIRECTIONS

1. In a medium saucepan over medium heat, mix together water, distilled white vinegar, white sugar, tomato paste, pineapple tidbits and cornstarch. Cook, stirring occasionally, 15 minutes, or until mixture reaches desired color and consistency.

BUTTERNUT SQUASH FRIES

Servings: 4 - Prep: 15m - Cooks: 20m - Total: 35m

NUTRITION FACTS

Calories: 102, Carbohydrates: 26.5g, Fat: 0.2g, Protein: 2.3g, Cholesterol: 0mg

INGREDIENTS

- 1 (2 pound) butternut squash, halved and seeded
- salt to taste

DIRECTIONS

1. Preheat the oven to 425 degrees F (220 degrees C).
2. Use a sharp knife to carefully cut away the peel from the squash. Cut the squash into sticks like French fries. Arrange squash pieces on a baking sheet and season with salt.
3. Bake for 20 minutes in the preheated oven, turning the fries over halfway through baking. Fries are done when they are starting to brown on the edges and become crispy.

UNSLOPPY JOES

Servings: 8 - Prep: 15m - Cooks: 15m - Total: 30m

NUTRITION FACTS

Calories: 204, Carbohydrates: 34.6g, Fat: 3.9g, Protein: 7.8g, Cholesterol: 0mg

INGREDIENTS

- 1 tablespoon olive oil
- 1 ½ tablespoons chili powder
- ½ cup chopped onion
- 1 tablespoon tomato paste
- ½ cup chopped celery
- 1 tablespoon distilled white vinegar
- ½ cup chopped carrots
- 1 teaspoon ground black pepper
- ½ cup chopped green bell pepper
- 1 (15 ounce) can kidney beans, drained and rinsed
- 1 clove garlic, minced
- 8 kaiser rolls
- 1 (14.5 ounce) can diced tomatoes

DIRECTIONS

1. Heat olive oil in a large skillet over medium heat. Add onion, celery, carrot, green pepper, and garlic: saute until tender. Stir in tomatoes, chili powder, tomato paste, vinegar, and pepper. Cover, reduce heat, and simmer 10 minutes.

2. Stir in kidney beans, and cook an additional 5 minutes.

3. Cut a 1/4 inch slice off the top of each kaiser roll; set aside. Hollow out the center of each roll, leaving about ½ inch thick shells; reserve the inside of rolls for other uses.

4. Spoon bean mixture evenly into rolls and replace tops. Serve immediately.

TERIYAKI AND PINEAPPLE CHICKEN

Servings: 8 - Prep: 15m - Cooks: 25m - Total: 40m

NUTRITION FACTS

Calories: 187, Carbohydrates: 18.1g, Fat: 5.5g, Protein: 16.3g, Cholesterol: 35mg

INGREDIENTS

- 2 tablespoons vegetable oil
- 1 onion, chopped
- 1 pound skinless, boneless chicken breasts, cut into cubes
- 1 cup teriyaki sauce
- 1 green bell pepper, sliced thin
- 1 (8 ounce) can pineapple chunks, undrained
- 1 yellow bell pepper, sliced thin
- 1 teaspoon garlic powder
- 1 red bell pepper, sliced thin
- 1 teaspoon crushed red pepper
- 1 1/4 cups sliced fresh mushrooms
- 1/4 cup all-purpose flour

DIRECTIONS

1. Heat the oil in a wok or large skillet over medium-high heat. Cook the chicken until no longer pink in the center and the juices run clear, 7 to 10 minutes.

2. Place the green bell pepper, yellow bell pepper, red bell pepper, mushrooms, onion, teriyaki sauce, pineapple chunks with the juice, garlic powder, and crushed red pepper into the wok, and turn the heat to medium. Bring to a simmer, stir in the flour, and continue simmering 15 minutes until thickened.

MEXICAN PASTA

Servings: 4 - Prep: 5m - Cooks: 15m - Total: 20m

NUTRITION FACTS

Calories: 358, Carbohydrates: 59.5g, Fat: 9.4g, Protein: 10.3g, Cholesterol: 0mg

INGREDIENTS

- ½ pound seashell pasta
- 1 (14.5 ounce) can peeled and diced tomatoes
- 2 tablespoons olive oil
- 1/4 cup salsa
- 2 onions, chopped
- 1/4 cup sliced black olives
- 1 green bell pepper, chopped
- 1 ½ tablespoons taco seasoning mix
- ½ cup sweet corn kernels
- salt and pepper to taste
- 1 (15 ounce) can black beans, drained

DIRECTIONS

1. Bring a large pot of lightly salted water to a boil. Add pasta and cook for 8 to 10 minutes or until al dente; drain.

2. While pasta is cooking, heat olive oil over medium heat in a large skillet. Cook onions and pepper in oil until lightly browned, 10 minutes. Stir in corn and heat through. Stir in black beans, tomatoes, salsa, olives, taco seasoning and salt and pepper and cook until thoroughly heated, 5 minutes.

3. Toss sauce with cooked pasta and serve.

FRESH SALSA

Servings: 48 - Prep: 20m - Cooks: 15m - Total: 35m

NUTRITION FACTS

Calories: 6, Carbohydrates: 1.5g, Fat: 0g, Protein: 0.2g, Cholesterol: 0mg

INGREDIENTS

- 4 jalapeno chile peppers
- 1 teaspoon salt
- 5 cloves garlic, finely chopped
- 1/4 teaspoon ground cumin
- 1 onion, finely chopped
- 1 (10 ounce) can diced tomatoes with green chile peppers
- 1 tablespoon white sugar
- 1 (28 ounce) can whole peeled tomatoes

DIRECTIONS

1. Preheat oven to 400 degrees F (200 degrees C).

2. Place jalapeno chile peppers on a medium baking sheet. Bake in the preheated oven 15 minutes, or until roasted. Remove from heat and chop off stems.

3. Place jalapeno chile peppers, garlic, onion, white sugar, salt, ground cumin and diced tomatoes with green chile peppers in a blender or food processor. Chop using the pulse setting for a few seconds. Mix in whole peeled tomatoes. Chop using the pulse setting to attain desired consistency. Transfer to a medium bowl. Cover and chill in the refrigerator until serving.

ROASTED VEGETABLE MEDLEY

Servings: 6 - Prep: 25m - Cooks: 1h - Total: 1h55m - Additional: 30m

NUTRITION FACTS

Calories: 191, Carbohydrates: 34.6g, Fat: 5g, Protein: 4g, Cholesterol: 0mg

INGREDIENTS

- 2 tablespoons olive oil, divided
- ½ cup roasted red peppers, cut into 1-inch pieces
- 1 large yam, peeled and cut into 1 inch pieces
- 2 cloves garlic, minced
- 1 large parsnip, peeled and cut into 1 inch pieces
- 1/4 cup chopped fresh basil
- 1 cup baby carrots
- ½ teaspoon kosher salt
- 1 zucchini, cut into 1 inch slices
- ½ teaspoon ground black pepper
- 1 bunch fresh asparagus, trimmed and cut into 1 inch pieces

DIRECTIONS

1. Preheat oven to 425 degrees F (220 degrees C). Grease 2 baking sheets with 1 tablespoon olive oil.
2. Place the yams, parsnips, and carrots onto the baking sheets. Bake in the preheated oven for 30 minutes, then add the zucchini and asparagus, and drizzle with the remaining 1 tablespoon of olive oil. Continue baking until all of the vegetables are tender, about 30 minutes more. Once tender, remove from the oven, and allow to cool for 30 minutes on the baking sheet.
3. Toss the roasted peppers together with the garlic, basil, salt, and pepper in a large bowl until combined. Add the roasted vegetables, and toss to mix. Serve at room temperature or cold.

ASPARAGUS, CHICKEN AND PENNE PASTA

Servings: 8 - Prep: 15m - Cooks: 20m - Total: 35m

NUTRITION FACTS

Calories: 311, Carbohydrates: 43.2g, Fat: 6.8g, Protein: 20.3g, Cholesterol: 29mg

INGREDIENTS

- 1 (16 ounce) package dry penne pasta
- 12 ounces asparagus, trimmed and cut into 1 inch pieces
- 2 tablespoons olive oil, divided
- 1 teaspoon crushed red pepper flakes
- 3⁄4pound skinless, boneless chicken breast meat - cut into bite-size pieces
- salt and pepper to taste
- 4 cloves garlic, minced
- ½ cup grated Parmesan cheese

DIRECTIONS

1. Bring a large pot of lightly salted water to a boil. Cook pasta in boiling water for 8 to 10 minutes, or until al dente. Drain, and transfer to a large bowl.
2. Heat 1 tablespoon olive oil in a large skillet over medium heat. Saute chicken until firm and lightly browned; remove from pan. Add the remaining tablespoon of olive oil to the skillet. Cook and stir garlic, asparagus, and red pepper flakes in oil until asparagus is tender. Stir in chicken, and cook for 2 minutes to blend the flavors. Season with salt and pepper.
3. Toss pasta with chicken and asparagus mixture. Sprinkle with Parmesan cheese.

FABULOUS FAJITAS

Servings: 10 - Prep: 15m - Cooks: 15m - Total: 30m

NUTRITION FACTS

Calories: 427, Carbohydrates: 64.2g, Fat: 10.3g, Protein: 18g, Cholesterol: 21mg

INGREDIENTS

- 2 green bell peppers, sliced
- 2 cups diced, cooked chicken meat
- 1 red bell pepper, sliced
- 1 (.7 ounce) package dry Italian-style salad dressing mix
- 1 onion, thinly sliced
- 10 (12 inch) flour tortillas
- 1 cup fresh sliced mushrooms

DIRECTIONS

1. Cut peppers and onion into thin slices. Do not dice, leave slices long and thin.
2. Saute peppers and onion in a small amount of oil until tender. Add mushrooms and chicken. Continue to cook on low heat until heated through. Stir in dry salad dressing mix and blend thoroughly.
3. Warm tortillas and roll mixture inside. If desired top with shredded cheddar cheese, diced tomato and shredded lettuce.

MARIA'S MEXICAN RICE

Servings: 6 - Prep: 10m - Cooks: 30m - Total: 40m

NUTRITION FACTS

Calories: 164, Carbohydrates: 26.8g, Fat: 4.9g, Protein: 2.7g, Cholesterol: 0mg

INGREDIENTS

- 2 tablespoons olive oil
- 1/8 teaspoon ground black pepper
- 1 cup rice
- 2 ½ cups water
- ½ large onion, diced
- 1/3 cup tomato sauce
- ½ tablespoon salt
- 1 tablespoon chicken bouillon (such as Knorr®)
- 1/8 teaspoon ground cumin
- 1 whole serrano chile pepper (optional)

DIRECTIONS

1. Heat oil in a saucepan over medium heat. Cook and stir rice and onion in the hot oil until browned, about 5 minutes; season with salt, cumin, and pepper. Pour water over the rice mixture. Stir tomato sauce and chicken bouillon into the water. Increase heat to medium-high, place a cover on the saucepan, and bring to a boil. Add serrano chile pepper and continue cooking at a boil for 10 minutes. Reduce heat to medium-low until the rice is tender and the water is absorbed, 15 to 20 minutes more.

PEPPERED BACON AND TOMATO LINGUINE

Servings: 6 - Prep: 15m - Cooks: 15m - Total: 30m

NUTRITION FACTS

Calories: 362, Carbohydrates: 57.5g, Fat: 7.6g, Protein: 16.2g, Cholesterol: 16mg

INGREDIENTS

- ½ pound peppered bacon, diced
- 1 teaspoon salt
- 2 tablespoons chopped green onion
- ground black pepper to taste
- 2 teaspoons minced garlic
- 1 (16 ounce) package linguine pasta
- 1 (14.5 ounce) can diced tomatoes

- 3 tablespoons grated Parmesan cheese
- 1 teaspoon dried basil

DIRECTIONS

1. Place bacon in a large, deep skillet. Cook over medium high heat until evenly brown. Drain, reserving drippings, and set aside.
2. Saute green onion and garlic in bacon drippings over medium heat for one minute. Stir in tomatoes, basil, salt and ground black pepper; simmer for 5 minutes.
3. Meanwhile, bring a large pot of lightly salted water to a boil. Add pasta and cook for 8 to 10 minutes or until al dente; drain.
4. Toss hot pasta with sauce and sprinkle with Parmesan cheese.

BAKED POTATO

Servings: 1 - Prep: 3m - Cooks: 1h30m - Total: 1h33m

NUTRITION FACTS

Calories: 128, Carbohydrates: 29.7g, Fat: 0.1g, Protein: 2.7g, Cholesterol: 0mg

INGREDIENTS

- 1 baking potato

DIRECTIONS

1. Preheat oven to 350 degrees F (175 degrees C).
2. Scrub the potato and prick it with a fork to prevent steam from building up and causing the potato to explode in your oven.
3. Bake for 1 ½ hours.

SLOW COOKER HOMEMADE BEANS

Servings: 12 - Prep: 20m - Cooks: 10h - Total: 10h20m

NUTRITION FACTS

Calories: 296, Carbohydrates: 57g, Fat: 3g, Protein: 12.4g, Cholesterol: 5mg

INGREDIENTS

- 3 cups dry navy beans, soaked overnight or boiled for one hour
- 1 tablespoon dry mustard
- 1 ½ cups ketchup
- 1 tablespoon salt
- 1 ½ cups water
- 6 slices thick cut bacon, cut into 1 inch pieces
- 1/4 cup molasses
- 1 cup brown sugar

- 1 large onion, chopped

DIRECTIONS

1. Drain soaking liquid from beans, and place them in a Slow Cooker.
2. Stir ketchup, water, molasses, onion, mustard, salt, bacon, and brown sugar into the beans until well mixed.
3. Cover, and cook on LOW for 8 to 10 hours, stirring occasionally if possible, though not necessary.

BUTTERNUT SQUASH PIZZAS WITH ROSEMARY

Servings: 4 - Prep: 20m - Cooks: 30m - Total: 50m

NUTRITION FACTS

Calories: 567, Carbohydrates: 96.9g, Fat: 13.7g, Protein: 14.8g, Cholesterol: 3mg

INGREDIENTS

- 1 cup thinly sliced onion
- 3 tablespoons olive oil, divided
- ½ butternut squash - peeled, seeded, and thinly sliced
- 1 (16 ounce) package refrigerated pizza crust dough, divided
- 1 teaspoon chopped fresh rosemary
- 1 tablespoon cornmeal
- salt and black pepper to taste
- 2 tablespoons grated Asiago or Parmesan cheese

DIRECTIONS

1. Preheat oven to 400 degrees F (205 degrees C). Place sliced onion and squash in a roasting pan. Sprinkle with rosemary, salt, pepper, and 2 tablespoons of the olive oil; toss to coat.
2. Bake in the preheated oven for 20 minutes, or until onions are lightly browned and squash is tender; set aside.
3. Increase oven temperature to 450 degrees F (230 degrees C). On a floured surface, roll each ball of dough into an 8 inch round. Place the rounds on a baking sheet sprinkled with cornmeal (you may need 2 baking sheets depending on their size). Distribute squash mixture over the two rounds and continue baking for 10 minutes, checking occasionally, or until the crust is firm. Sprinkle with cheese and remaining tablespoon olive oil. Cut into quarters, and serve.

CHICKEN AND BROCCOLI PASTA

Servings: 8 - Prep: 10m - Cooks: 10m - Total: 20m

NUTRITION FACTS

Calories: 368, Carbohydrates: 51g, Fat: 7.7g, Protein: 23.5g, Cholesterol: 34mg

INGREDIENTS

- 3 tablespoons olive oil
- salt and pepper to taste
- 1 pound skinless, boneless chicken breast halves - cut into 1 inch pieces
- 1 pinch dried oregano
- 1 tablespoon chopped onion
- 18 ounces dry penne pasta
- 2 cloves garlic, chopped
- 1/4 cup fresh basil leaves, cut into thin strips
- 2 (14.5 ounce) cans diced tomatoes
- 2 tablespoons grated Parmesan cheese
- 2 cups fresh broccoli florets

DIRECTIONS

1. In a large skillet over medium heat, warm oil and add chicken; cook until slightly brown. Add onion and garlic to cook for about 5 minutes or until garlic is golden and onions are translucent.
2. Add tomatoes, broccoli, salt, pepper and oregano; stir well and bring to a boil. Cover and turn down heat to simmer for about 10 minutes.
3. Meanwhile, bring a large pot of lightly salted water to a boil. Add pasta and cook for 8 to 10 minutes or until tender; drain and add back into pot. Pour chicken sauce into pot and mix well.
4. Add basil and toss well; top with Parmesan cheese. Serve.

LEMONY QUINOA

Servings: 6 - Prep: 15m - Cooks: 10m - Total: 25m

NUTRITION FACTS

Calories: 147, Carbohydrates: 21.4g, Fat: 4.8g, Protein: 5.9g, Cholesterol: 0mg

INGREDIENTS

- 1/4 cup pine nuts
- 2 stalks celery, chopped
- 1 cup quinoa
- 1/4 red onion, chopped
- 2 cups water
- 1/4 teaspoon cayenne pepper
- sea salt to taste
- ½ teaspoon ground cumin
- 1/4 cup fresh lemon juice

- 1 bunch fresh parsley, chopped

DIRECTIONS

1. Toast the pine nuts briefly in a dry skillet over medium heat. This will take about 5 minutes, and stir constantly as they will burn easily. Set aside to cool.
2. In a saucepan, combine the quinoa, water and salt. Bring to a boil, then reduce heat to medium and cook until quinoa is tender and water has been absorbed, about 10 minutes. Cool slightly, then fluff with a fork.
3. Transfer the quinoa to a serving bowl and stir in the pine nuts, lemon juice, celery, onion, cayenne pepper, cumin and parsley. Adjust salt and pepper if needed before serving.

FROZEN VEGETABLE STIR-FRY

Servings: 6 - Prep: 5m - Cooks: 5m - Total: 10m

NUTRITION FACTS

Calories: 88, Carbohydrates: 13.8g, Fat: 2.9g, Protein: 3.5g, Cholesterol: 0mg

INGREDIENTS

- 2 tablespoons soy sauce
- 2 teaspoons peanut butter
- 1 tablespoon brown sugar
- 2 teaspoons olive oil
- 2 teaspoons garlic powder
- 1 (16 ounce) package frozen mixed vegetables

DIRECTIONS

1. Combine soy sauce, brown sugar, garlic powder, and peanut butter in a small bowl.
2. Heat oil in a large skillet over medium heat; cook and stir frozen vegetables until just tender, 5 to 7 minutes. Remove from heat and fold in soy sauce mixture.

SLOW COOKER BALSAMIC CHICKEN

Servings: 6 - Prep: 15m - Cooks: 4h - Total: 4h15m

NUTRITION FACTS

Calories: 200, Carbohydrates: 17.6g, Fat: 6.8g, Protein: 18.6g, Cholesterol: 43mg

INGREDIENTS

- 2 tablespoons olive oil
- 1 teaspoon dried basil
- 4 skinless, boneless chicken breast halves, or more to taste
- 1 teaspoon dried rosemary
- salt and ground black pepper to taste

- ½ teaspoon dried thyme
- 1 onion, thinly sliced
- ½ cup balsamic vinegar
- 4 cloves garlic
- 2 (14.5 ounce) cans crushed tomatoes
- 1 teaspoon dried oregano

DIRECTIONS

1. Drizzle olive oil into the slow cooker. Place chicken breasts on top of oil and season each breast with salt and pepper. Top chicken breasts with onion slices, garlic, oregano, basil, rosemary, and thyme. Drizzle balsamic vinegar over seasoned breasts and pour tomatoes on top.
2. Cook in the slow cooker set to High until chicken is no longer pink in the center and the juices run clear, about 4 hours.

ZUCCHINI COOKIES

Servings: 36 - Prep: 15m - Cooks: 10m - Total: 25m

NUTRITION FACTS

Calories: 81, Carbohydrates: 13.4g, Fat: 2.7g, Protein: 1g, Cholesterol: 5mg

INGREDIENTS

- ½ cup margarine, softened
- 1 teaspoon baking soda
- 1 cup white sugar
- ½ teaspoon salt
- 1 egg
- 1 teaspoon ground cinnamon
- 1 cup grated zucchini
- ½ teaspoon ground cloves
- 2 cups all-purpose flour
- 1 cup raisins

DIRECTIONS

1. In a medium bowl, cream together the margarine and sugar until smooth. Beat in the egg then stir in the zucchini. Combine the flour, baking soda, salt and cinnamon; stir into the zucchini mixture. Mix in raisins. Cover dough and chill for at least 1 hour or overnight.
2. Preheat oven to 375 degrees F (190 degrees C). Grease cookie sheets. Drop dough by teaspoonfuls onto the prepared cookie sheet. Cookies should be about 2 inches apart.
3. Bake for 8 to 10 minutes in the preheated oven until set. Allow cookies to cool slightly on the cookie sheets before removing to wire racks to cool completely.

MY FAVORITE SESAME NOODLES

Servings: 1 - Prep: 10m - Cooks: 15m - Total: 25m

NUTRITION FACTS

Calories: 787, Carbohydrates: 114.6g, Fat: 26.1g, Protein: 28.3g, Cholesterol: 0mg

INGREDIENTS

- ½ (8 ounce) package spaghetti
- 1 teaspoon sesame oil
- 2 tablespoons peanut butter
- 1 teaspoon ground ginger
- 1 tablespoon honey
- 1 clove garlic, minced
- 2 tablespoons tamari
- 1 green onion, chopped
- 1 teaspoon Thai chili sauce
- 2 teaspoons sesame seeds

DIRECTIONS

1. Fill a large pot with lightly salted water and bring to a rolling boil over high heat. Once the water is boiling, stir in the spaghetti, and return to a boil. Cook the pasta uncovered, stirring occasionally, until the pasta has cooked through, but is still firm to the bite, about 12 minutes. Drain well in a colander set in the sink.

2. Melt the peanut butter in a large microwave-safe glass or ceramic bowl, 15 to 20 seconds (depending on your microwave). Whisk the honey, tamari, and chili sauce into the peanut butter, then stir in the sesame oil and ginger. Mix in the garlic and green onions and toss with the spaghetti. Top with the sesame seeds.

GARLIC CHICKEN FRIED BROWN RICE

Servings: 3 - Prep: 20m - Cooks: 15m - Total: 35m

NUTRITION FACTS

Calories: 444, Carbohydrates: 57.4g, Fat: 12.8g, Protein: 24.3g, Cholesterol: 43mg

INGREDIENTS

- 2 tablespoons vegetable oil, divided
- 3 cups cooked brown rice
- 8 ounces skinless, boneless chicken breast, cut into strips
- 2 tablespoons light soy sauce
- ½ red bell pepper, chopped
- 1 tablespoon rice vinegar

- ½ cup green onion, chopped
- 1 cup frozen peas, thawed
- 4 cloves garlic, minced

DIRECTIONS

1. Heat 1 tablespoon of vegetable oil in a large skillet set over medium heat. Add the chicken, bell pepper, green onion and garlic. Cook and stir until the chicken is cooked through, about 5 minutes. Remove the chicken to a plate and keep warm.
2. Heat the remaining tablespoon of oil in the same skillet over medium-high heat. Add the rice; cook and stir to heat through. Stir in the soy sauce, rice vinegar and peas, and continue to cook for 1 minute. Return the chicken mixture to the skillet and stir to blend with the rice and heat through before serving.

EASY MASOOR DAAL

Servings: 4 - Prep: 5m - Cooks: 30m - Total: 35m

NUTRITION FACTS

Calories: 185, Carbohydrates: 25g, Fat: 5.2g, Protein: 11.1g, Cholesterol: 0mg

INGREDIENTS

- 1 cup red lentils
- ½ teaspoon cayenne pepper, or to taste
- 1 slice ginger, 1 inch piece, peeled
- 4 teaspoons vegetable oil
- 1/4 teaspoon ground turmeric
- 4 teaspoons dried minced onion
- 1 teaspoon salt
- 1 teaspoon cumin seeds

DIRECTIONS

1. Rinse lentils thoroughly and place in a medium saucepan along with ginger, turmeric, salt and cayenne pepper. Cover with about 1 inch of water and bring to a boil. Skim off any foam that forms on top of the lentils. Reduce heat and simmer, stirring occasionally, until beans are tender and soupy.
2. Meanwhile, in a microwave safe dish combine oil, dried onion and cumin seeds. Microwave on high for 45 seconds to 1 minute; be sure to brown, but not burn, onions. Stir into lentil mixture.

THAI SPICY BASIL CHICKEN FRIED RICE

Servings: 6 - Prep: 30m - Cooks: 10m - Total: 40m

NUTRITION FACTS

Calories: 794, Carbohydrates: 116.4g, Fat: 22.1g, Protein: 29.1g, Cholesterol: 46mg

INGREDIENTS

- 3 tablespoons oyster sauce
- 1 pound boneless, skinless chicken breast, cut into thin strips
- 2 tablespoons fish sauce
- 1 red pepper, seeded and thinly sliced
- 1 teaspoon white sugar
- 1 onion, thinly sliced
- ½ cup peanut oil for frying
- 2 cups sweet Thai basil
- 4 cups cooked jasmine rice, chilled
- 1 cucumber, sliced (optional)
- 6 large cloves garlic clove, crushed
- ½ cup cilantro sprigs (optional)
- 2 serrano peppers, crushed

DIRECTIONS

1. Whisk together the oyster sauce, fish sauce, and sugar in a bowl.
2. Heat the oil in a wok over medium-high heat until the oil begins to smoke. Add the garlic and serrano peppers, stirring quickly. Stir in the chicken, bell pepper, onion and oyster sauce mixture; cook until the chicken is no longer pink. Raise heat to high and stir in the chilled rice; stir quickly until the sauce is blended with the rice. Use the back of a spoon to break up any rice sticking together.
3. Remove from heat and mix in the basil leaves. Garnish with sliced cucumber and cilantro as desired.

CAVATELLI AND BROCCOLI

Servings: 12 - Prep: 10m - Cooks: 25m - Total: 35m

NUTRITION FACTS

Calories: 317, Carbohydrates: 47.6g, Fat: 10.3g, Protein: 10.2g, Cholesterol: 1mg

INGREDIENTS

- 3 heads fresh broccoli, cut into florets
- 1 teaspoon salt
- ½ cup olive oil
- 1 teaspoon crushed red pepper flakes
- 3 cloves garlic, minced
- 2 tablespoons grated Parmesan cheese
- 1 ½ pounds cavatelli pasta

DIRECTIONS

1. In a large pot of boiling water, blanch broccoli for about 5 minutes. Drain, and set aside.

2. Heat olive oil in a large skillet over medium heat. Saute garlic until lightly golden, being careful not to burn it. Add the broccoli. Saute, stirring occasionally, for about 10 minutes. Broccoli should be tender yet crisp to the bite.

3. Meanwhile, cook cavatelli in a large pot of boiling salted water for 8 to 10 minutes, or until al dente. Drain, and place in a large serving bowl. Toss with the broccoli, and season with salt and hot pepper flakes. Serve with parmesan cheese.

ALBINO PASTA

Servings: 8 - Prep: 15m - Cooks: 10m - Total: 25m

NUTRITION FACTS

Calories: 275, Carbohydrates: 41g, Fat: 9g, Protein: 8.8g, Cholesterol: 3mg

INGREDIENTS

- 1 (16 ounce) package dry penne pasta
- 1 teaspoon minced garlic
- 4 tablespoons olive oil
- 1/3 cup grated Parmesan cheese

DIRECTIONS

1. Bring a large pot of lightly salted water to a boil. Add penne pasta and cook for 8 to 10 minutes or until al dente; drain.

2. In small saucepan, saute garlic a small amount of oil. Combine garlic, olive oil, and pasta in a bowl. Mix in parmesan cheese.

PASTA HOT! HOT! HOT!

Servings: 4 - Prep: 15m - Cooks: 15m - Total: 30m

NUTRITION FACTS

Calories: 561, Carbohydrates: 84.8g, Fat: 16.7g, Protein: 16.7g, Cholesterol: 4mg

INGREDIENTS

- 1 (16 ounce) package spaghetti
- ½ teaspoon crushed red pepper
- 1/4 cup olive oil
- 1/4 cup grated Parmesan cheese
- 3 cloves garlic, chopped

DIRECTIONS

1. Bring a large pot of lightly salted water to a boil. Add pasta and cook for 8 to 10 minutes or until al dente; drain.

2. In a small saucepan over low heat place olive oil, garlic and peppers and simmer. Pour olive oil mixture over cooked pasta and serve with Parmesan cheese.

RICE WITH BLACK BEANS

Servings: 8 - Prep: 5m - Cooks: 15m - Total: 20m

NUTRITION FACTS

Calories: 80, Carbohydrates: 14.4g, Fat: 2g, Protein: 1.6g, Cholesterol: 0mg

INGREDIENTS

- 1 onion, chopped
- ½ teaspoon dried oregano
- 1 tablespoon vegetable oil
- ½ teaspoon garlic powder
- 1 (14.5 ounce) can stewed tomatoes
- 1 cup instant white rice
- 1 (15 ounce) can black beans, undrained

DIRECTIONS

1. In a large saucepan, cook and stir onion in oil until tender and translucent, but not brown. Add tomatoes, beans, oregano and garlic powder. Bring to boil. Stir in rice, return mixture to a boil. Reduce heat to simmer, and cover.

2. Let mixture simmer for 5 minutes. Remove pan from heat and let stand 5 minutes before serving.

CINNAMON AND LIME CHICKEN FAJITAS

Servings: 6 - Prep: 15m - Cooks: 40m - Total: 55m

NUTRITION FACTS

Calories: 395, Carbohydrates: 49.5g, Fat: 12.9g, Protein: 22.3g, Cholesterol: 45mg

INGREDIENTS

- 4 boneless, skinless chicken breast halves
- 1 large yellow onion, chopped
- 1 tablespoon ground cinnamon
- 1 large clove garlic, peeled and minced
- salt and pepper to taste
- 1 tablespoon chopped jalapeno peppers
- 2 large baking potatoes, peeled and cubed
- 1 lime, juiced
- ¼ cup canola oil
- 12 (6 inch) corn tortillas, warmed

DIRECTIONS

1. Preheat oven to 400 degrees F (200 degrees C).

2. Place potatoes in a shallow baking dish. Drizzle with about ½ the oil, and season with salt. Bake 30 to 40 minutes in the preheated oven, until tender.

3. Meanwhile, season chicken with cinnamon, salt, and pepper. Arrange in a separate baking dish, and bake 30 minutes in the preheated oven, until no longer pink and juices run clear. Cool and shred.

4. Heat remaining oil in a skillet over medium heat, and saute onion and garlic until tender. Mix in shredded chicken, jalapeno, and lime juice. Cook until heated through.

5. Serve the chicken and potatoes in warmed tortillas.

HARD CANDY

Servings: 36 - Prep: 5m - Cooks: 25m - Total: 45m

NUTRITION FACTS

Calories: 124, Carbohydrates: 32.2g, Fat: 0g, Protein: 0g, Cholesterol: 0mg

INGREDIENTS

- 3   3⁄4cups white sugar
- 1 tablespoon orange, or other flavored extract
- 1 ½ cups light corn syrup
- ½ teaspoon food coloring (optional)
- 1 cup water
- 1/4 cup confectioners' sugar for dusting

DIRECTIONS

1. In a medium saucepan, stir together the white sugar, corn syrup, and water. Cook, stirring, over medium heat until sugar dissolves, then bring to a boil. Without stirring, heat to 300 to 310 degrees F (149 to 154 degrees C), or until a small amount of syrup dropped into cold water forms hard, brittle threads.

2. Remove from heat and stir in flavored extract and food coloring, if desired. Pour onto a greased cookie sheet, and dust the top with confectioners' sugar. Let cool, and break into pieces. Store in an airtight container.

QUINOA BREAKFAST PUDDING

Servings: 6 - Prep: 5m - Cooks: 35m - Total: 40m

NUTRITION FACTS

Calories: 202, Carbohydrates: 42.6g, Fat: 1.9g, Protein: 4.4g, Cholesterol: 0mg

INGREDIENTS

- 1 cup quinoa
- 2 tablespoons lemon juice
- 2 cups water
- 1 teaspoon ground cinnamon, or to taste
- 2 cups apple juice

- salt to taste
- 1 cup raisins
- 2 teaspoons vanilla extract

DIRECTIONS

1. Place quinoa in a sieve and rinse thoroughly. Allow to drain, then place quinoa in a medium saucepan with water. Bring to a boil over high heat. Cover pan with lid, lower heat, and allow to simmer until all water is absorbed and quinoa is tender, about 15 minutes.
2. Mix in apple juice, raisins, lemon juice, cinnamon, and salt. Cover pan and allow to simmer for 15 minutes longer. Stir in vanilla extract. Serve warm.

ROASTED VEGETABLE ORZO

Servings: 4 - Prep: 25m - Cooks: 20m - Total: 45m

NUTRITION FACTS

Calories: 621, Carbohydrates: 104.5g, Fat: 11.4g, Protein: 24.9g, Cholesterol: 3mg

INGREDIENTS

- 1 zucchini, sliced
- 1 pinch white sugar
- 1 summer squash, sliced
- salt and black pepper to taste
- 1 red onion, cut into chunks
- 4 cubes chicken bouillon
- 1 pound asparagus, cut into 1-inch pieces
- 1/4 cup dry white wine
- 1 pound portobello mushrooms, thickly sliced
- 1 (16 ounce) package orzo pasta
- 4 cloves garlic, minced
- 2 tablespoons grated Parmesan cheese
- 2 tablespoons olive oil

DIRECTIONS

1. Preheat oven to 450 degrees F (230 degrees C).
2. Place the zucchini, squash, onion, asparagus, and mushrooms in a large bowl; add in garlic, olive oil and sugar, and stir gently to coat vegetables. Spread vegetables in a single layer on a baking sheet, and sprinkle with salt and pepper.
3. Roast vegetables until tender, 20 to 25 minutes.
4. Meanwhile, bring a large pot of lightly salted water to boil. Add bouillon cubes, wine, and orzo, and cook until al dente, about 8 to 10 minutes. Drain. Stir in roasted vegetables and Parmesan cheese, and serve warm.

PESTO PASTA

Servings: 8 - Prep: 5m - Cooks: 10m - Total: 15m

NUTRITION FACTS

Calories: 225, Carbohydrates: 32g, Fat: 7.2g, Protein: 7.8g, Cholesterol: 44mg

INGREDIENTS

- ½ cup chopped onion
- 1 (16 ounce) package pasta
- 2 ½ tablespoons pesto
- salt to taste
- 2 tablespoons olive oil
- ground black pepper to taste
- 2 tablespoons grated Parmesan cheese

DIRECTIONS

1. Cook pasta in a large pot of boiling water until done. Drain.

2. Meanwhile, heat the oil in a frying pan over medium low heat. Add pesto, onion, and salt and pepper. Cook about five minutes, or until onions are soft.

3. In a large bowl, mix pesto mixture into pasta. Stir in grated cheese. Serve.

MIKE'S HOMEMADE PIZZA

Servings: 8 - Prep: 1h10m - Cooks: 20m - Total: 1h30m

NUTRITION FACTS

Calories: 239, Carbohydrates: 41.3g, Fat: 5.6g, Protein: 6.2g, Cholesterol: 0mg

INGREDIENTS

- 1 (.25 ounce) envelope active dry yeast
- 1 teaspoon salt
- 1 cup lukewarm water
- 1/8 teaspoon ground black pepper
- 3 cups all-purpose flour
- 1/4 teaspoon garlic powder
- 1/4 teaspoon salt
- 1/4 teaspoon dried basil
- 2 tablespoons shortening
- ½ teaspoon dried oregano
- 1 tablespoon vegetable oil
- 1/4 teaspoon dried marjoram

- ½ cup chopped onion
- 1/4 teaspoon ground cumin
- 1 (6 ounce) can tomato paste
- 1/4 teaspoon chili powder
- 6 fluid ounces water
- 1/8 teaspoon crushed red pepper flakes
- ½ teaspoon white sugar

DIRECTIONS

1. In a small bowl, dissolve yeast in warm water. Let stand until creamy, about 10 minutes.
2. In a large bowl, combine flour, salt and shortening. Stir in the yeast mixture. When the dough has pulled together, turn it out onto a lightly floured surface, and knead until smooth and elastic, about 8 minutes. Lightly oil a large bowl, place the dough in the bowl, and turn to coat with oil. Cover with a damp cloth, and let rise in a warm place until doubled in volume, about 45 minutes.
3. Heat oil in a small saucepan over medium heat. Saute onion until tender. Stir in tomato paste and water. Season with sugar, salt, black pepper, garlic powder, basil, oregano, marjoram, cumin, chili powder and red pepper flakes. Simmer 15 to 20 minutes.
4. Recipe makes 2 (12 inch) pizzas. Divide dough in half, and spread onto pizza pans. Cover with sauce, and desired toppings. Bake at 400 degrees for 20 minutes, or until crust is golden brown.

EASY LIMA BEANS

Servings: 6 - Prep: 15m - Cooks: 30m - Total: 45m

NUTRITION FACTS

Calories: 84, Carbohydrates: 15.9g, Fat: 0g, Protein: 4.1g, Cholesterol: 0mg

INGREDIENTS

- cooking spray
- 1 ½ cups chicken broth
- ½ medium onion, finely chopped
- 1 (16 ounce) package frozen baby lima beans

DIRECTIONS

1. Heat a large saucepan over medium heat, and spray with cooking spray. Saute onions until soft and translucent. Pour in chicken broth, and bring to a boil. Add lima beans, and enough water just to cover. Bring to a boil, then reduce heat to low, cover, and simmer for 30 minutes, until beans are tender.

DOREEN'S HAM SLICES ON THE GRILL

Servings: 4 - Prep: 10m - Cooks: 15m - Total: 25m

NUTRITION FACTS

Calories: 245, Carbohydrates: 58g, Fat: 1.3g, Protein: 2.7g, Cholesterol: 8mg

INGREDIENTS

- 1 cup packed brown sugar
- 1/3 cup prepared horseradish
- 1/4 cup lemon juice
- 2 slices ham

DIRECTIONS

1. Preheat an outdoor grill for high heat and lightly oil grate.
2. In a small bowl, mix brown sugar, lemon juice and prepared horseradish.
3. Heat the brown sugar mixture in the microwave on high heat 1 minute, or until warm.
4. Score both sides of ham slices. Place on the prepared grill. Baste continuously with the brown sugar mixture while grilling. Grill 6 to 8 minutes per side, or to desired doneness.

BROKEN SPAGHETTI RISOTTO

Servings: 2 - Prep: 10m - Cooks: 15m - Total: 25m

NUTRITION FACTS

Calories: 518, Carbohydrates: 86.3g, Fat: 10.5g, Protein: 17.8g, Cholesterol: 9mg

INGREDIENTS

- 1 tablespoon olive oil
- ½ teaspoon red pepper flakes, or to taste
- 8 ounces uncooked spaghetti, broken into 1 inch pieces
- salt to taste
- 2 cloves garlic, minced
- 2 tablespoons freshly grated Parmigiano-Reggiano cheese, or to taste
- 1 ½ cups chicken broth
- 1 tablespoon chopped fresh flat-leaf parsley

DIRECTIONS

1. Heat oil in a saucepan over medium heat; add spaghetti and toast, stirring constantly, until golden brown, 3 to 5 minutes.
2. Stir garlic into spaghetti pieces and cook for 30 seconds.
3. Pour in ½ cup broth and increase heat to medium high. Stir spaghetti and broth until all the liquid is absorbed, 2 to 3 minutes. Repeat this process until all of the stock is absorbed and noodles are desired tenderness, about 10 minutes.
4. Reduce heat to low. Season spaghetti with salt and red pepper flakes to taste. Remove from heat.
5. Stir Parmigiano-Reggiano cheese and parsley into spaghetti and serve.

EASY LIMA BEANS

Servings: 6 - Prep: 15m - Cooks: 30m - Total: 45m

NUTRITION FACTS

Calories: 84, Carbohydrates: 15.9g, Fat: 0g, Protein: 4.1g, Cholesterol: 0mg

INGREDIENTS

- cooking spray
- 1 ½ cups chicken broth
- ½ medium onion, finely chopped
- 1 (16 ounce) package frozen baby lima beans

DIRECTIONS

1. Heat a large saucepan over medium heat, and spray with cooking spray. Saute onions until soft and translucent. Pour in chicken broth, and bring to a boil. Add lima beans, and enough water just to cover. Bring to a boil, then reduce heat to low, cover, and simmer for 30 minutes, until beans are tender.

CHICKEN YAKISOBA

Servings: 4 - Prep: 20m - Cooks: 15m - Total: 35m

NUTRITION FACTS

Calories: 503, Carbohydrates: 69.8g, Fat: 16.5g, Protein: 26.5g, Cholesterol: 29mg

INGREDIENTS

- 2 tablespoons canola oil
- ½ medium head cabbage, thinly sliced
- 1 tablespoon sesame oil
- 1 onion, sliced
- 2 skinless, boneless chicken breast halves - cut into bite-size pieces
- 2 carrots, cut into matchsticks
- 2 cloves garlic, minced
- 1 tablespoon salt
- 2 tablespoons Asian-style chile paste
- 2 pounds cooked yakisoba noodles
- ½ cup soy sauce
- 2 tablespoons pickled ginger, or to taste (optional)
- 1 tablespoon canola oil

DIRECTIONS

1. Heat 2 tablespoons canola oil and sesame oil in a large skillet over medium-high heat. Cook and stir chicken and garlic in hot oil until fragrant, about 1 minute. Stir chile paste into chicken mixture; cook and stir until chicken is completely browned, 3 to 4 minutes. Add soy sauce and simmer for 2 minutes. Pour chicken and sauce into a bowl.
2. Heat 1 tablespoon canola oil in the skillet over medium-high heat; cook and stir cabbage, onion, carrots, and salt in hot oil until cabbage is wilted, 3 to 4 minutes.

3. Stir the chicken mixture into the cabbage mixture. Add noodles; cook and stir until noodles are hot and chicken is no longer pink inside, 3 to 4 minutes. Garnish with pickled ginger.

ZUCCHINI WITH CHICKPEA AND MUSHROOM STUFFING

Servings: 8 - Prep: 30m - Cooks: 30m - Total: 1h

NUTRITION FACTS

Calories: 107, Carbohydrates: 18.4g, Fat: 2.7g, Protein: 4.5g, Cholesterol: 0mg

INGREDIENTS

- 4 zucchini, halved
- 1 ½ teaspoons ground cumin, or to taste
- 1 tablespoon olive oil
- 1 (15.5 ounce) can chickpeas, rinsed and drained
- 1 onion, chopped
- ½ lemon, juiced
- 2 cloves garlic, crushed
- 2 tablespoons chopped fresh parsley
- ½ (8 ounce) package button mushrooms, sliced
- sea salt to taste
- 1 teaspoon ground coriander
- ground black pepper to taste

DIRECTIONS

1. Preheat oven to 350 degrees F (175 degrees C). Grease a shallow baking dish.
2. Scoop out the flesh of the zucchini; chop the flesh and set aside. Place the shells in the prepared dish.
3. Heat oil in a large skillet over medium heat. Saute onions for 5 minutes, then add garlic and saute 2 minutes more. Stir in chopped zucchini and mushrooms; saute 5 minutes. Stir in coriander, cumin, chickpeas, lemon juice, parsley, salt and pepper. Spoon mixture into zucchini shells.
4. Bake in preheated oven for 30 to 40 minutes, or until zucchini are tender.

LENTIL RICE AND VEGGIE BAKE

Servings: 6 - Prep: 15m - Cooks: 1h - Total: 1h15m

NUTRITION FACTS

Calories: 187, Carbohydrates: 35.1g, Fat: 1.5g, Protein: 9.7g, Cholesterol: 0mg

INGREDIENTS

- ½ cup uncooked long grain white rice
- 1/3 cup chopped carrots

- 2 ½ cups water
- 1/3 cup chopped zucchini
- 1 cup red lentils
- 1 (8 ounce) can tomato sauce
- 1 teaspoon vegetable oil
- 1 teaspoon dried basil
- 1 small onion, chopped
- 1 teaspoon dried oregano
- 3 cloves garlic, minced
- 1 teaspoon ground cumin
- 1 fresh tomato, chopped
- salt and pepper to taste
- 1/3 cup chopped celery

DIRECTIONS

1. Place the rice and 1 cup water in a pot, and bring to a boil. Cover, reduce heat to low, and simmer 20 minutes. Place lentils in a pot with the remaining 1 ½ cups water, and bring to a boil. Cook 15 minutes, or until tender.

2. Preheat oven to 350 degrees F (175 degrees C).

3. Heat the oil in a skillet over medium heat, and stir in the onion and garlic. Mix in tomato, celery, carrots, zucchini, and ½ the tomato sauce. Season with ½ the basil, ½ the oregano, ½ the cumin, salt, and pepper. Cook until vegetables are tender.

4. In a casserole dish, mix the rice, lentils, and vegetables. Top with remaining tomato sauce, and sprinkle with remaining basil, oregano, and cumin.

5. Bake 30 minutes in the preheated oven, until bubbly.

MEXICAN QUINOA

Servings: 4 - Prep: 20m - Cooks: 20m - Total: 40m

NUTRITION FACTS

Calories: 244, Carbohydrates: 38.1g, Fat: 6.1g, Protein: 8.1g, Cholesterol: 2mg

INGREDIENTS

- 1 tablespoon olive oil
- 1 (10 ounce) can diced tomatoes with green chile peppers (such as RO*TEL®)
- 1 cup quinoa, rinsed
- 1 envelope gluten-free taco seasoning mix
- 1 small onion, chopped
- 2 cups low-sodium chicken broth
- 2 cloves garlic, minced

- 1/4 cup chopped fresh cilantro
- 1 jalapeno pepper, seeded and chopped (optional)

DIRECTIONS

1. Heat olive oil in a large skillet over medium heat; cook and stir quinoa and onion in the hot oil until onion is translucent, about 5 minutes. Add garlic and jalapeno pepper to quinoa mixture and cook until garlic is fragrant and slightly softened, 1 or 2 more minutes.
2. Mix undrained can of diced tomatoes with green chiles, taco seasoning mix, and chicken broth into quinoa mixture. Bring to a boil, reduce heat to medium-low, and simmer until liquid has been absorbed, 15 to 20 minutes. Stir in cilantro.

HONEY SOY TILAPIA

Servings: 2 - Prep: 10m - Cooks: 15m - Total: 55m

NUTRITION FACTS

Calories: 218, Carbohydrates: 33.3g, Fat: 1.4g, Protein: 19.4g, Cholesterol: 31mg

INGREDIENTS

- 3 tablespoons honey
- 2 (3 ounce) fillets tilapia
- 3 tablespoons soy sauce
- cooking spray
- 3 tablespoons balsamic vinegar
- 1 teaspoon freshly cracked black pepper
- 1 tablespoon minced garlic

DIRECTIONS

1. Mix the honey, soy sauce, balsamic vinegar, and garlic together in a bowl. Place the tilapia fillets in the mixture; allow to marinate in refrigerator at least 30 minutes.
2. Preheat an oven to 350 degrees F (175 degrees C). Spray a baking dish with cooking spray.
3. Remove tilapia from marinade, and discard the marinade. Place fillets into the prepared baking sheet, and sprinkle the black pepper over the fish.
4. Bake in the preheated oven until the fish flakes easily with a fork, 15 to 20 minutes.

SPICY MANGO SWEET POTATO CHICKEN

Servings: 5 - Prep: 30m - Cooks: 20m - Total: 50m

NUTRITION FACTS

Calories: 268, Carbohydrates: 30.2g, Fat: 7.5g, Protein: 21.1g, Cholesterol: 47mg

INGREDIENTS

- 2 cups cubed peeled sweet potatoes

- 3 tablespoons honey
- 2 tablespoons vegetable oil
- 3 tablespoons hot sauce, or to taste
- 1 pound skinless, boneless chicken breast halves - cubed
- 1 ripe mango, peeled and cubed
- 1 clove garlic, minced
- 1/4 teaspoon crushed red pepper flakes
- 6 tablespoons tamari soy sauce
- 1 teaspoon cornstarch
- 3/4cup water
- 1 tablespoon warm water

DIRECTIONS

1. Place the sweet potatoes into a saucepan and fill with enough water to cover. Simmer over medium-high heat until tender, about 15 minutes. Drain and set aside.

2. Meanwhile, heat 2 tablespoons of vegetable oil in a skillet over medium-high heat. Stir in chicken, and cook until no longer pink in the center, about 5 minutes; set aside. Stir garlic into the skillet, and cook for a few minutes, until fragrant. Pour in the tamari, 3/4cup of water, honey, and hot sauce. Bring to a simmer, then stir in the sweet potato, chicken, mango, and red pepper flakes. Cook and stir until hot. Dissolve the cornstarch in 1 tablespoon of water, and stir into the simmering mixture; stir until thickened.

SIMPLE BAKED BEANS

Servings: 10 - Prep: 15m - Cooks: 3h - Total: 3h15m

NUTRITION FACTS

Calories: 176, Carbohydrates: 31.7g, Fat: 3.9g, Protein: 5.6g, Cholesterol: 10mg

INGREDIENTS

- 2 (16 ounce) cans baked beans with pork
- 1 tablespoon prepared mustard
- 1/4 cup molasses
- 2 tablespoons ketchup
- 1/4 cup chopped onions
- 2 slices bacon, chopped
- 4 tablespoons brown sugar

DIRECTIONS

1. Preheat oven to 350 degrees F (175 degrees C).

2. Mix baked beans with pork, molasses, onions, brown sugar and ketchup together and put in a greased casserole dish. Top with bacon, cover and bake for 3 hours or until thick.

FRIED ZUCCHINI

Servings: 4 - Prep: 20m - Cooks: 20m - Total: 40m

NUTRITION FACTS

Calories: 195, Carbohydrates: 31.1g, Fat: 6.2g, Protein: 4.4g, Cholesterol: 0mg

INGREDIENTS

- 2 zucchini, quartered and sliced
- ½ teaspoon salt
- 1 onion, sliced into rings
- ½ teaspoon ground black pepper
- ½ cup all-purpose flour
- 1/4 teaspoon garlic powder
- ½ cup cornmeal
- 1 cup vegetable oil for frying

DIRECTIONS

1. Place zucchini and onions in a medium bowl and mix together.
2. In a small bowl mix flour, cornmeal, salt, pepper and garlic powder.
3. Pour dry mixture over zucchini/onion mixture, cover bowl and shake well. Let mixture sit for about 30 minutes; a batter will form on the vegetables.
4. In a medium skillet heat oil over medium heat. When oil is hot add breaded vegetables and fry, turning to brown evenly.

SALSA DE TOMATILLO

Servings: 16 - Prep: 20m - Cooks: 10m - Total: 30m

NUTRITION FACTS

Calories: 10, Carbohydrates: 2g, Fat: 0.2g, Protein: 0.3g, Cholesterol: 0mg

INGREDIENTS

- 10 tomatillos, husked
- 2 jalapeno peppers, chopped
- 1 small onion, chopped
- 1/4 cup chopped fresh cilantro
- 3 cloves garlic, chopped
- salt and pepper to taste

DIRECTIONS

1. Place tomatillos in a nonreactive saucepan with enough water to cover. Bring to a boil. Simmer until tomatillos soften and begin to burst, about 10 minutes.

2. Drain tomatillos and place in a food processor or blender with onion, garlic, jalapeno peppers, cilantro, salt and pepper. Blend to desired consistency.

SWEET CHILI THAI SAUCE

Servings: 24 - Prep: 15m - Cooks: 5m - Total: 20m

NUTRITION FACTS

Calories: 34, Carbohydrates: 8.7g, Fat: 0g, Protein: 0g, Cholesterol: 0mg

INGREDIENTS

- 1 cup water
- 1 teaspoon garlic, minced
- 1 cup rice vinegar
- 2 teaspoons hot chile pepper, minced
- 1 cup sugar
- 2 teaspoons ketchup
- 2 teaspoons fresh ginger root, minced
- 2 teaspoons cornstarch

DIRECTIONS

1. Pour water and vinegar into a saucepan, and bring to a boil over high heat. Stir in sugar, ginger, garlic, chile pepper, and ketchup; simmer for 5 minutes. Stir in cornstarch. Remove saucepan from stove to cool. Then transfer to a bowl, cover, and refrigerate until needed.

SPINACH, RED LENTIL, AND BEAN CURRY

Servings: 4 - Prep: 25m - Cooks: 10m - Total: 35m

NUTRITION FACTS

Calories: 328, Carbohydrates: 51.9g, Fat: 8.3g, Protein: 18g, Cholesterol: 2mg

INGREDIENTS

- 1 cup red lentils
- 1 onion, chopped
- 1/4 cup tomato puree
- 2 cloves garlic, chopped
- ½ (8 ounce) container plain yogurt
- 1 (1 inch) piece fresh ginger root, grated
- 1 teaspoon garam masala
- 4 cups loosely packed fresh spinach, coarsely chopped
- ½ teaspoon ground dried turmeric
- 2 tomatoes, chopped

- ½ teaspoon ground cumin
- 4 sprigs fresh cilantro, chopped
- ½ teaspoon ancho chile powder
- 1 (15.5 ounce) can mixed beans, rinsed and drained
- 2 tablespoons vegetable oil

DIRECTIONS

1. Rinse lentils and place in a saucepan with enough water to cover. Bring to a boil. Reduce heat to low, cover pot, and simmer over low heat for 20 minutes. Drain.

2. In a bowl, stir together tomato puree and yogurt. Season with garam masala, turmeric, cumin, and chile powder. Stir until creamy.

3. Heat oil in a skillet over medium heat. Stir in onion, garlic, and ginger; cook until onion begins to brown. Stir in spinach; cook until dark green and wilted. Gradually stir in yogurt mixture. Then mix in tomatoes and cilantro.

4. Stir lentils and mixed beans into mixture until well combined. Heat through, about 5 minutes.

QUICK SESAME GREEN BEANS

Servings: 4 - Prep: 10m - Cooks: 5m - Total: 15m

NUTRITION FACTS

Calories: 45, Carbohydrates: 7.1g, Fat: 1.4g, Protein: 2.3g, Cholesterol: 0mg

INGREDIENTS

- 8 ounces fresh green beans, trimmed
- 4 cloves garlic, minced
- 2 tablespoons low sodium soy sauce
- 1 teaspoon grated fresh ginger root
- ½ tablespoon miso paste
- 1 tablespoon sesame seeds, toasted
- ½ teaspoon red pepper flakes

DIRECTIONS

1. Place the green beans into a steamer insert and set in a pot over one inch of water. Bring to a boil, cover and steam for 5 minutes. Remove from the heat and transfer beans to a serving bowl.

2. Meanwhile, in a small bowl, stir together the soy sauce, miso paste, red pepper flakes, garlic and ginger. Pour over the green beans and toss to coat. Sprinkle sesame seeds on top.

EMILY'S FAMOUS MARSHMALLOWS

Servings: 18 - Prep: 30m - Cooks: 20m - Total: 8h40m

NUTRITION FACTS

Calories: 118, Carbohydrates: 29.8g, Fat: 0g, Protein: 0.4g, Cholesterol: 0mg

INGREDIENTS

- 1 cup confectioners' sugar for dusting
- 4 tablespoons unflavored gelatin
- 2 cups white sugar
- 2 egg whites
- 1 tablespoon light corn syrup
- 1 teaspoon vanilla extract
- 1 1/4 cups water, divided

DIRECTIONS

1. Dust a 9x9 inch square dish generously with confectioners' sugar.
2. In a small saucepan over medium-high heat, stir together white sugar, corn syrup and   3⁄4cup water. Heat to 250 to 265 degrees F (121 to 129 degrees C), or until a small amount of syrup dropped into cold water forms a rigid ball. ☐ While syrup is heating, place remaining water in a metal bowl and sprinkle gelatin over the surface. Place bowl over simmering water until gelatin has dissolved completely. Keep in a warm place until syrup has come to temperature. Remove syrup from heat and whisk gelatin mixture into hot syrup. Set aside.
3. In a separate bowl, whip egg whites to soft peaks. Continue to beat, pouring syrup mixture into egg whites in a thin stream, until the egg whites are very stiff. Stir in vanilla. Spread evenly in prepared pan and let rest 8 hours or overnight before cutting.

PINTO BEANS WITH MEXICAN-STYLE SEASONINGS

Servings: 8 - Prep: 15m - Cooks: 4h - Total: 12h15m - Additional: 8h

NUTRITION FACTS

Calories: 267, Carbohydrates: 40.9g, Fat: 5.2g, Protein: 16.4g, Cholesterol: 10mg

INGREDIENTS

- 1 pound dried pinto beans, rinsed
- 1 tablespoon ground cumin, or to taste
- 2 (10 ounce) cans diced tomatoes with green chile peppers (such as RO*TEL®)
- 1 ½ teaspoons garlic powder, or to taste
- ½ pound bacon, cut into ½-inch pieces
- ½ bunch fresh cilantro, chopped
- 1 yellow onion, chopped
- salt to taste
- 1 tablespoon chili powder, or to taste

DIRECTIONS

1. Place pinto beans into a large pot and pour in enough water to cover by 2 to 3 inches. Let beans soak overnight.
2. Drain beans, return to pot, and pour in fresh water to cover; add diced tomatoes, bacon, onion, chili powder, cumin, and garlic powder. Bring to a boil, reduce heat to low, and simmer for 3 hours.
3. Stir cilantro and salt into bean mixture; simmer until beans are soft, about 1 more hour.

GRILLED BAKED POTATOES

Servings: 6 - Prep: 5m - Cooks: 25m - Total: 30m

NUTRITION FACTS

Calories: 194, Carbohydrates: 35.8g, Fat: 4.7g, Protein: 1.6g, Cholesterol: 0mg

INGREDIENTS

- 4 large baking potatoes, quartered
- 2 teaspoons garlic powder
- 2 tablespoons olive oil
- 2 teaspoons dried rosemary
- 2 teaspoons freshly ground black pepper
- salt to taste

DIRECTIONS

1. Place the potatoes into a large pot with water to cover. Bring to a boil and cook over medium-high heat for about 10 minutes, or until tender.
2. Preheat the grill to medium-high heat. Drain potatoes and toss with olive oil, black pepper, rosemary and salt to taste.
3. Place the potatoes skin-side down over indirect heat on the grill and reserve liquid. Grill for about 15 minutes. Remove potatoes to a serving plate and sprinkle with the reserved olive oil mixture.

HALIBUT WITH RICE WINE

Servings: 6 - Prep: 20m - Cooks: 40m - Total: 1h

NUTRITION FACTS

Calories: 194, Carbohydrates: 8.6g, Fat: 4.3g, Protein: 23.9g, Cholesterol: 36mg

INGREDIENTS

- 1 teaspoon vegetable oil
- 1 tablespoon rice vinegar
- 1 shallots, finely chopped
- 6 (4 ounce) fillets halibut, skin removed
- 2 cloves garlic, finely chopped
- 1 teaspoon sesame oil
- 1 tablespoon black bean sauce

- 1/4 teaspoon pepper
- ½ cup mirin (Japanese sweet wine)
- 2 tablespoons chopped fresh cilantro
- 1 tablespoon soy sauce

DIRECTIONS

1. Heat oil in non-stick saucepan over medium heat. Cook shallots and garlic gently until fragrant, but not brown. Stir in black bean sauce, rice wine, and soy sauce. Bring to boil and cook until reduced by half. Remove from heat, and stir in vinegar; set aside.
2. Pat fish dry. Rub with sesame oil and sprinkle with pepper. Preheat an outdoor grill for high heat, and lightly oil grate.
3. Grill fish for about 5 minutes per side, or just until cooked through. Sprinkle with cilantro. Serve with sauce poured over top.

SAVORY ROASTED ROOT VEGETABLES

Servings: 6 - Prep: 30m - Cooks: 45m - Total: 1h15m

NUTRITION FACTS

Calories: 143, Carbohydrates: 20.8g, Fat: 4.9g, Protein: 2.8g, Cholesterol: 0mg

INGREDIENTS

- 1 cup diced, raw beet
- 2 tablespoons olive oil
- 4 carrots, diced
- 1 tablespoon dried thyme leaves
- 1 onion, diced
- salt and pepper to taste
- 2 cups diced potatoes
- 1/3 cup dry white wine
- 4 cloves garlic, minced
- 1 cup torn beet greens
- 1/4 cup canned garbanzo beans (chickpeas), drained

DIRECTIONS

1. Preheat an oven to 400 degrees F (200 degrees C).
2. Place the beet, carrot, onion, potatoes, garlic, and garbanzo beans into a 9x13 inch baking dish. Drizzle with the olive oil, then season with thyme, salt, and pepper. Mix well.
3. Bake, uncovered, in the preheated oven for 30 minutes, stirring once midway through baking. Remove the baking dish from the oven, and stir in the wine. Return to the oven, and bake until the wine has mostly evaporated and the vegetables are tender, about 15 minutes more. Stir in the beet greens, allowing them to wilt from the heat of the vegetables. Season to taste with salt and pepper before serving.

HARVARD BEETS

Servings: 3 - Prep: 5m - Cooks: 10m - Total: 15m

NUTRITION FACTS

Calories: 207, Carbohydrates: 53.1g, Fat: 0g, Protein: 0.1g, Cholesterol: 0mg

INGREDIENTS

- 1 (16 ounce) can beets
- 1 tablespoon cornstarch
- ½ cup white vinegar
- salt to taste
- 3⁄4cup white sugar

DIRECTIONS

1. Drain the beet liquid into a medium saucepan. To the liquid add vinegar, sugar, cornstarch and salt. Bring to a boil over medium-high heat. Reduce heat to medium; stir in beets and cook until heated through.

CANDIED APPLES

Servings: 15 - Prep: 10m - Cooks: 30m - Total: 40m

NUTRITION FACTS

Calories: 237, Carbohydrates: 62.5g, Fat: 0.2g, Protein: 0.4g, Cholesterol: 0mg

INGREDIENTS

- 15 apples
- 1 ½ cups water
- 2 cups white sugar
- 8 drops red food coloring
- 1 cup light corn syrup

DIRECTIONS

1. Lightly grease cookie sheets. Insert craft sticks into whole, stemmed apples.

2. In a medium saucepan over medium-high heat, combine sugar, corn syrup and water. Heat to 300 to 310 degrees F (149 to 154 degrees C), or until a small amount of syrup dropped into cold water forms hard, brittle threads. Remove from heat and stir in food coloring.

3. Holding apple by its stick, dip in syrup and remove and turn to coat evenly. Place on prepared sheets to harden.

ANAHEIM FISH TACOS

Servings: 6 - Prep: 15m - Cooks: 30m - Total: 45m

NUTRITION FACTS

Calories: 273, Carbohydrates: 29.9g, Fat: 5.1g, Protein: 27.7g, Cholesterol: 36mg

INGREDIENTS

- 1 teaspoon vegetable oil
- 2 large tomatoes, diced
- 1 Anaheim chile pepper, chopped
- ½ teaspoon ground cumin
- 1 leek, chopped
- 1 ½ pounds halibut fillets
- 2 cloves garlic, crushed
- 1 lime
- salt and pepper to taste
- 12 corn tortillas
- 1 cup chicken broth

DIRECTIONS

1. Heat the oil in a large skillet over medium heat, and saute the chile, leek, and garlic until tender and lightly browned. Season with salt and pepper.
2. Mix the chicken broth and tomatoes into the skillet, and season with cumin. Bring to a boil. Reduce heat to low. Place the halibut into the mixture. Sprinkle with lime juice. Cook 15 to 20 minutes until the halibut is easily flaked with a fork. Wrap in warmed corn tortillas to serve.

HAM & PICCALILLI SALAD

Prep: 15 mins No cook

Serves 4

INGREDIENTS

- 4 tbsp piccalilli
- 3 tbsp natural yogurt

12 silverskin pickled onions, halved

- 130g pea shoots
- 180g pulled ham hock or shredded cooked ham

½ cucumber, halved and thickly sliced

- 100g fresh peas

40g mature cheddar, shaved

crusty bread, to serve

METHOD

STEP 1

Mix the piccalilli, yogurt, onions and 4 tbsp water together to make a dressing. Season and set aside.

STEP 2

Toss the pea shoots, ham, cucumber and peas together. Pile onto a serving plate, then drizzle over the dressing. Top with the cheese and serve with crusty bread.

AVOCADO & BEAN TRIANGLES

Prep:5 mins No cook

Serves 2

INGREDIENTS

- 3 triangluar bread thins

210g can red kidney beans, drained

1 tbsp finely chopped dill, plus extra for garnish

1/2 lemon, for squeezing

1 tomato, chopped

- 1 small avocado

1 small red onion, finely chopped

METHOD

STEP 1

Follow our triangular bread thins recipe to make your own. While they bake, roughly mash the beans with the dill and a good squeeze of lemon then stir in the tomato.

STEP 2

Cut the bread triangles in half and top with the beans. Scoop the avocado into a bowl and roughly mash with a squeeze more lemon. Spoon the avocado onto the beans, scatter over the chopped onion, then garnish with the remaining dill.

SUMMER CARROT, TARRAGON & WHITE BEAN SOUP

Prep:10 mins **Cook:**20 mins

Serves 4

INGREDIENTS

- 1 tbsp rapeseed oil

2 large leeks, well washed, halved lengthways and finely sliced

700g carrots, chopped

- 1.4l hot reduced-salt vegetable bouillon (we used Marigold)

4 garlic cloves, finely grated

- 2 x 400g cans cannellini beans in water

⅔ small pack tarragon, leaves roughly chopped

METHOD

STEP 1

Heat the oil over a medium heat in a large pan and fry the leeks and carrots for 5 mins to soften.

STEP 2

Pour over the stock, stir in the garlic, the beans with their liquid, and three-quarters of the tarragon, then cover and simmer for 15 mins or until the veg is just tender. Stir in the remaining tarragon before serving.

.

THAI FRIED PRAWN & PINEAPPLE RICE

Prep:10 mins **Cook:**15 mins

Serves 4

INGREDIENTS

- 2 tsp sunflower oil

bunch spring onions, greens and whites separated, both sliced

1 green pepper, deseeded and chopped into small chunks

140g pineapple, chopped into bite-sized chunks

- 3 tbsp Thai green curry paste

4 tsp light soy sauce, plus extra to serve

- 300g cooked basmati rice (brown, white or a mix - about 140g uncooked rice)

2 large eggs, beaten

- 140g frozen peas

225g can bamboo shoots, drained

250g frozen prawns, cooked or raw

2-3 limes, 1 juiced, the rest cut into wedges to serve

- handful coriander leaves (optional)

METHOD

STEP 1

Heat the oil in a wok or non-stick frying pan and fry the spring onion whites for 2 mins until softened. Stir in the pepper for 1 min, followed by the pineapple for 1 min more, then stir in the green curry paste and soy sauce.

STEP 2

Add the rice, stir-frying until piping hot, then push the rice to one side of the pan and scramble the eggs on the other side. Stir the peas, bamboo shoots and prawns into the rice and eggs, then heat through for 2 mins until the prawns are hot and the peas tender. Finally, stir in the spring onion greens, lime juice and coriander, if using. Spoon into bowls and serve with extra lime wedges and soy sauce.

FETA & CLEMENTINE LUNCH BOWL

Prep:15 mins **Cook:**15 mins

Serves 2

INGREDIENTS

1 red onion, halved and thinly sliced

1 lemon, zested and juiced

2 clementines, 1 zested, flesh sliced

2 garlic cloves, chopped

400g can green lentils, drained

- 1 tbsp balsamic vinegar
- 1 ½ tbsp rapeseed oil

1 red pepper, quartered and sliced

60g feta, crumbled

small handful mint, chopped

4 walnut halves, chopped

METHOD

STEP 1

Mix the onion with the lemon juice, lemon and clementine zest and garlic.

STEP 2

Tip the lentils into two bowls or lunchboxes and drizzle over the balsamic and 1 tbsp oil. Heat the remaining oil in a large non-stick wok, add the pepper and stir-fry for 3 mins. Tip in half the onion and cook until tender. Pile on top of the lentils, then mix the clementines, remaining onions, feta, mint and walnut pieces.

CARROT & GINGER SOUP

Prep:15 mins **Cook:**25 mins - 30 mins

Serves 4

INGREDIENTS

- 1 tbsp rapeseed oil
- 1 large onion, chopped
- 2 tbsp coarsely grated ginger
- 2 garlic cloves, sliced
- ½ tsp ground nutmeg
- 850ml vegetable stock
- 500g carrot (preferably organic), sliced
- 400g can cannellini beans (no need to drain)

Supercharged topping

- 4 tbsp almonds in their skins, cut into slivers
- sprinkle of nutmeg

METHOD

STEP 1

Heat the oil in a large pan, add the onion, ginger and garlic, and fry for 5 mins until starting to soften. Stir in the nutmeg and cook for 1 min more.

STEP 2

Pour in the stock, add the carrots, beans and their liquid, then cover and simmer for 20-25 mins until the carrots are tender.

STEP 3

Scoop a third of the mixture into a bowl and blitz the remainder with a hand blender or in a food processor until smooth. Return everything to the pan and heat until bubbling. Serve topped with the almonds and nutmeg.

FRENCH TOAST BACON BUTTIES

Prep:5 mins **Cook:**25 mins

Serves 2

INGREDIENTS

- 2 eggs
- 180ml milk
- 1 tbsp caster sugar
- 4 slices white bread
- 2 tbsp butter
- 4 rashers back bacon, grilled
- icing sugar and syrup of choice (we like date syrup), to serve

METHOD

STEP 1

Whisk the eggs and milk with the sugar in a bowl. Soak the white sliced bread in the mixture.

STEP 2

Heat 1 tbsp of the butter in a non-stick frying pan and fry two slices of the soaked bread on a low–medium heat until golden and crisp, about 3–4 mins on each side. Remove from the pan and sandwich 2 slices of bacon between the slices of French toast. Repeat with the remaining soaked bread to make the other sandwich.

STEP 3

Serve with a dusting of icing sugar and a drizzle of syrup.

MISO MUSHROOM & TOFU NOODLE SOUP

Prep:10 mins **Cook:**15 mins

Serves 1

INGREDIENTS

- 1 tbsp rapeseed oil

70g mixed mushrooms, sliced

50g smoked tofu, cut into small cubes

- ½ tbsp brown rice miso paste
- 50g dried buckwheat or egg noodles

2 spring onions, shredded

METHOD

STEP 1

Heat half the oil in a frying pan over a medium heat. Add the mushrooms and fry for 5-6 mins, or until golden. Transfer to a bowl using a slotted spoon and set aside. Add the remaining oil to the pan and fry the tofu for 3-4 mins, or until evenly golden.

STEP 2

Mix the miso paste with 325ml boiling water in a jug. Cook the noodles following pack instructions, then drain and transfer to a bowl. Top with the mushrooms and tofu, then pour over the miso broth. Scatter over the spring onions just before serving.

WHITE VELVET SOUP WITH SMOKY ALMONDS

Prep:10 mins **Cook:**25 mins

Serves 2

INGREDIENTS

- 2 tsp rapeseed oil

2 large garlic cloves, sliced

2 leeks, trimmed so they're mostly white in colour, washed well, then sliced (about 240g)

200g cauliflower, chopped

- 2 tsp vegetable bouillon powder

400g cannellini beans, rinsed

fresh nutmeg, for grating

- 100ml whole milk

25g whole almonds, chopped

- ½ tsp smoked paprika

2 x 25g slices rye bread, to serve

METHOD

STEP 1

Heat the oil in a large pan. Add the garlic, leeks and cauliflower and cook for about 5 mins, stirring frequently, until starting to soften (but not colouring).

STEP 2

Stir in the vegetable bouillon and beans, pour in 600ml boiling water and add a few generous gratings of the nutmeg. Cover and leave to simmer for 15 mins until the leeks and cauliflower are tender. Add the milk and blitz with a hand blender until smooth and creamy.

STEP 3

Put the almonds in a dry pan and cook very gently for 1 min, or until toasted, then remove from the heat. Scatter the paprika over the almonds and mix well. Ladle the soup into bowls, top with the spicy nuts and serve with the rye bread.

POLISH APPLE CAKE (SZARLOTKA)

Prep:35 mins **Cook:**1 hr plus freezing

Serves 12

INGREDIENTS

For the filling

- half a lemon
- 6 large Bramley or cooking apples
- 4 tbsp soft brown sugar
- 1 tbsp ground cinnamon

For the dough

450g plain flour, plus extra for dusting

- 1 tsp baking powder

200g unsalted butter, cut into pieces, plus extra for greasing

- 225g golden caster sugar

3 egg yolks, plus 1 whole egg, at room temperature

- 1 tbsp natural yogurt
- 1 tbsp lemon zest (from the half a lemon, above)
- 1 tsp vanilla extract

To serve

icing sugar, for dusting

- 300ml pot whipping cream
- 1 tsp cinnamon

METHOD

STEP 1

Heat oven to 180C/160C fan/gas 4. Grease and line a 20 x 29cm baking tray with baking parchment.

STEP 2

For the filling, zest the lemon half and leave aside for the dough. Peel, core and thinly slice the apples, then squeeze over the juice of the lemon to stop the fruit turning brown. Put the apples in a large pan and add the sugar, 200ml water and cinnamon. Cook for 5 mins, then remove from the heat and leave to cool in the liquid (you'll need this later).

STEP 3

To make the dough, put the flour and baking powder in a food processor or into a large bowl and pulse or stir to combine. Add the butter and mix again until the mixture is sandy. Add the sugar, egg yolks and egg, yogurt, lemon zest and vanilla extract and mix into a dough. Tip it out onto a floured surface. Bring it together with your hands and roll it into a ball.

STEP 4

Split the dough in half, wrap one half in cling film and freeze for 1 hr. Roll out the other dough half so that it is big enough to fill the bottom of the lined tray. With the palm of your hand, push the dough about halfway up the sides of the tray until the whole base is covered. Prick the dough with a fork and bake in the oven for about 15 mins until it is golden and lightly springy to the touch.

STEP 5

Spoon over the apple filling, with about half the cooking liquid, then set aside.

STEP 6

Remove the dough from the freezer and coarsely grate, as you would a block of cheese. Sprinkle the grated dough over the apples and bake for 40-45 mins until it is golden and the topping has cooked through. Leave to cool completely, dust with icing sugar, then cut into squares. Whip the cream until thick, stir in the cinnamon and serve alongside the cake.

VEGAN BOLOGNESE

Prep:20 mins **Cook:**1 hr

Serves 3

INGREDIENTS

- 15g dried porcini mushrooms
- 1 ½ tbsp olive oil
- ½ onion, finely chopped
- 1 carrot, finely chopped
- 1 celery stick, finely chopped
- 2 garlic cloves, sliced
- 2 thyme sprigs
- ½ tsp tomato purée
- 50ml vegan red wine (optional)
- 125g dried green lentils
- 400g can whole plum tomatoes
- 125g chestnut mushrooms, chopped
- 125g portobello mushrooms, sliced
- ½ tsp soy sauce
- ½ tsp Marmite
- 270g spaghetti
- handful fresh basil leaves

METHOD

STEP 1

Pour 400ml boiling water over the dried porcini and leave for 10 mins until hydrated. Meanwhile pour 1 tbsp oil into a large saucepan. Add the onion, carrot, celery and a pinch of salt. Cook gently, stirring for 10 mins until soft. Remove the porcini from the liquid, keeping the mushroomy stock and roughly chop. Set both aside.

STEP 2

Add the garlic and thyme to the pan. Cook for 1 min then stir in the tomato purée and cook for a min more. Pour in the red wine, if using, cook until nearly reduced, then add the lentils, reserved mushroom stock and tomatoes. Bring to the boil, then reduce the heat and leave to simmer with a lid on.

STEP 3

Meanwhile, heat a large frying pan. Add the remaining oil, then tip in the chestnut, portobello and rehydrated mushrooms. Fry until all the water has evaporated and the mushrooms are deep golden brown. Pour in the soy sauce. Give everything a good mix, then scrape the mushrooms into the lentil mixture.

STEP 4

Stir in the Marmite and continue to cook the ragu, stirring occasionally, over a low-medium heat for 30-45 mins until the lentils are cooked and the sauce is thick and reduced, adding extra water if necessary. Remove the thyme sprigs and season to taste.

STEP 5

Cook the spaghetti in a large pan of salted water for 1 min less than packet instructions. Drain the pasta, reserving a ladleful of pasta water, then toss the spaghetti in the sauce, using a little of the starchy liquid to loosen up the ragu slightly so that the pasta clings to the sauce. Serve topped with fresh basil and some black pepper.

SIMPLE SUGAR ROSES

Total time1 hr Takes 1 hour per batch. no cook

Makes 40 roses and leaves

INGREDIENTS

edible food colouring paste (we used Claret and Party Green)

200g ready-to-roll icing

a little solid vegetable fat, for rolling (see Know-how below)

edible lustre (we used a shimmery pink), optional

edible sparkles (we used bright pink), optional

METHOD

STEP 1

Start with the roses. Knead a little of the colouring paste into 150g of the icing until pale and even. Break into three balls, then add a little more colouring to two, giving three varying depths of colour. Keep under cling film. Rub a very thin layer of fat over a smooth work surface. Roll out one of the balls of icing thinly, about 1-2mm, then trim into a rectangle about 8 x 20cm. Cut off a 1cm strip of icing widthways, keeping the rest covered.

STEP 2

Carefully roll the icing up and around itself. For a more realistic rose look, start rolling slightly skew-whiff so that the outside edge of the finished rose sticks out further than the middle. With about 2cm to go, start to guide the end of the icing down and under to make a neat rosebud. Pinch to shape, then cut or pinch off the bottom. Set aside for at least 1 hr until firm. Repeat with the rest of the icing.

STEP 3

For the leaves, colour the remaining icing green. Pinch off small pea-size pieces, roll into balls, then flatten a little. Pinch one end to make a leaf shape. Leave to dry.

STEP 4

Once the roses are dry and firm, dust a little lustre onto each rose using a paintbrush or your fingertip. Sprinkle with sparkles, if using. Position the roses onto the cupcakes in clusters of three, following with three leaves. You'll need 36 leaves and roses for 12 cakes.

AVOCADO & STRAWBERRY SMOOTHIE

Prep:5 mins No cook

Serves 2

INGREDIENTS

½ avocado, stoned, peeled and cut into chunks

150g strawberry, halved

- 4 tbsp low-fat natural yogurt
- 200ml semi-skimmed milk

lemon or lime juice, to taste

honey, to taste

METHOD

STEP 1

Put all the INGREDIENTS in a blender and whizz until smooth. If the consistency is too thick, add a little water.

SAMOSA PIE

Prep:5 mins **Cook:**30 mins

Serves 4

INGREDIENTS

* 2-3 tbsp vegetable oil

1 onion, chopped

* 500g lamb mince

2 garlic cloves, finely chopped

* 2 tbsp curry powder
* 1 large sweet potato (about 300g), peeled and grated
* 100g frozen peas

handful coriander, roughly chopped

* juice 0.5 lemon
* 3-4 sheets filo pastry
* 1 tsp cumin seeds

METHOD

STEP 1

Heat oven to 180C/160C fan/gas 4. Heat 1 tbsp of the oil in a frying pan. Cook the onion and mince for about 5 mins until the meat is browned. Stir in the garlic, curry powder, sweet potato and 300ml water. Cook for 5-8 mins until the potato has softened. Stir in the peas, coriander and a squeeze of lemon juice, then season.

STEP 2

Spoon the mixture into a baking dish. Brush the sheets of filo with the remaining oil and scrunch over the top of the mince. Sprinkle with cumin seeds and bake for 10-15 mins or until the top is crisp.

GOOSEBERRY CRÈME BRÛLÉE TART

Prep:10 mins **Cook:**1 hr and 20 mins

Serves 8

INGREDIENTS

- 450g gooseberries
- 200g white caster sugar
- 4 eggs
- 100ml double cream
- 500g block sweet pastry

flour, for dusting

METHOD

STEP 1

Tip the gooseberries into a saucepan with 100g of the sugar and 100ml water. Simmer for 8-10 mins until the fruit is soft and the juices are syrupy. Tip the fruit into a sieve set over a jug and leave to strain – you will need about 150ml of the syrupy juices. Tip the pulp into a bowl and leave to cool.

STEP 2

In a separate bowl, beat the eggs with 50g of the sugar, then beat in the cream and gooseberry syrup. Strain through a sieve into another jug and set aside.

STEP 3

Heat oven to 160C/140C fan/gas 3. Roll out the pastry on a lightly floured surface to the thickness of a £1 coin, then lift into a 23cm tart tin. Press down gently on the bottom and sides, leaving a slight overhang. Line the tart with foil and fill with baking beans. Bake for 10 mins, then discard the foil and beans, and bake for another 20 mins. Remove from the oven and leave to cool.

STEP 4

Reduce oven to 150C/130C fan/gas 2. Spread the pulp evenly over the base of the tart, then carefully pour the cream mixture over it to create 2 layers. Bake for 35-40 mins until the cream layer has the slightest wobble to it. Remove from the oven and trim the pastry edges. Leave to cool completely, then scatter over the remaining sugar, caramelise with a blowtorch, if you like, and serve straight away.

SPINACH CHICKPEA CURRY

Servings: 4 - Prep: 5m - Cooks: 15m - Total: 20m

NUTRITION FACTS

Calories: 346, Carbohydrates: 44.7g, Fat: 12.3g, Protein: 21.7g, Cholesterol: 0mg

INGREDIENTS

- 1 tablespoon vegetable oil
- ½ teaspoon garlic powder, or to taste
- 1 onion, chopped
- 1 (15 ounce) can garbanzo beans (chickpeas), drained and rinsed
- 1 (14.75 ounce) can creamed corn
- 1 (12 ounce) package firm tofu, cubed
- 1 tablespoon curry paste
- 1 bunch fresh spinach, stems removed
- salt to taste
- 1 teaspoon dried basil or to taste
- ground black pepper to taste

DIRECTIONS

1. In a large wok or skillet heat oil over medium heat; saute onions until translucent. Stir in creamed corn and curry paste. Cook, stirring regularly, for 5 minutes. As you stir, add salt, pepper and garlic.
2. Stir in garbanzo beans and gently fold in tofu. Add spinach and cover. When spinach is tender, remove from heat and stir in basil.

SCALLOP SCAMPI

Servings: 8 - Prep: 15m - Cooks: 30m - Total: 45m

NUTRITION FACTS

Calories: 360, Carbohydrates: 43.5g, Fat: 9.3g, Protein: 21.3g, Cholesterol: 31mg

INGREDIENTS

- 4 tablespoons margarine
- ½ cup grated Romano cheese
- 3 cloves garlic, minced
- 1 (10.75 ounce) can chicken broth
- 1 large onion, minced
- 1 pound bay scallops
- ½ cup dry white wine
- 1 pound linguine pasta

- 1 teaspoon salt
- 1/4 cup chopped fresh parsley
- 1/4 teaspoon ground black pepper

DIRECTIONS

1. In a large skillet, melt margarine over medium heat and saute garlic and onion until translucent. Add wine, salt, ground black pepper and 1/4 cup cheese.
2. Add chicken broth and scallops; increase heat and boil rapidly for 7 to 8 minutes.
3. Meanwhile, bring a large pot of lightly salted water to a boil. Add pasta and cook for 8 to 10 minutes or until al dente; drain.
4. Reduce heat for scallop mixture and add parsley; place sauce on top of linguine. Sprinkle with remaining cheese; serve.

APPLESAUCE

Servings: 4 - Prep: 20m - Cooks: 15m - Total: 35m

NUTRITION FACTS

Calories: 195, Carbohydrates: 51g, Fat: 0.3g, Protein: 0.5g, Cholesterol: 0mg

INGREDIENTS

- 6 cups apples - peeled, cored and chopped
- 1/8 teaspoon ground cloves
- 3/4 cup water
- ½ cup white sugar
- 1/8 teaspoon ground cinnamon

DIRECTIONS

1. In a 2 quart saucepan over medium heat, combine apples, water, cinnamon, and cloves. Bring to a boil, reduce heat, and simmer 10 minutes. Stir in sugar, and simmer 5 more minutes.
1. v allow to sit at least 30 minutes before serving.

BLACKENED TILAPIA WITH SECRET HOBO SPICES

Servings: 4 - Prep: 10m - Cooks: 8m - Total: 18m

NUTRITION FACTS

Calories: 245, Carbohydrates: 21.5g, Fat: 6.8g, Protein: 26.8g, Cholesterol: 42mg

INGREDIENTS

- 3 tablespoons paprika
- 1 teaspoon dried thyme

- 1 tablespoon onion powder
- ½ teaspoon celery seed
- 1 pinch garlic powder
- 1 tablespoon kosher salt, or to taste
- 1 teaspoon ground white pepper
- 1 pound tilapia fillets
- 1 teaspoon ground black pepper
- 1 lemon, cut into wedges
- 1 teaspoon cayenne pepper, or to taste
- 4 slices white bread
- 1 teaspoon dried oregano
- 1 tablespoon vegetable oil

DIRECTIONS

1. In a small bowl or jar with a lid, make the spice blend. Mix together the paprika, onion powder, garlic powder, white pepper, black pepper, cayenne pepper, oregano, thyme, celery seed and kosher salt. Coat the fish fillets with the spice mixture, and allow to sit at room temperature for no longer than 30 minutes.

2. Heat a heavy skillet over high heat. Add oil, and heat until it is almost smoking. Place the fillets in the pan, and cook for about 3 minutes per side, or until fish is opaque and can be flaked with a fork. Remove from the pan, and place onto slices of white bread. Pour pan juices over them and squeeze lemon juice all over. Do not underestimate the white bread. It gets quite tasty soaking up all the juices.

PERFECT SUSHI RICE

Servings: 15 - Prep: 5m - Cooks: 20m - Total: 25m

NUTRITION FACTS

Calories: 112, Carbohydrates: 23.5g, Fat: 1g, Protein: 1.7g, Cholesterol: 0mg

INGREDIENTS

- 2 cups uncooked glutinous white rice (sushi rice)
- 1 tablespoon vegetable oil
- 3 cups water
- 1/4 cup white sugar
- ½ cup rice vinegar
- 1 teaspoon salt

DIRECTIONS

1. Rinse the rice in a strainer or colander until the water runs clear. Combine with water in a medium saucepan. Bring to a boil, then reduce the heat to low, cover and cook for 20 minutes. Rice should be tender and water should be absorbed. Cool until cool enough to handle.

2. In a small saucepan, combine the rice vinegar, oil, sugar and salt. Cook over medium heat until the sugar dissolves. Cool, then stir into the cooked rice. When you pour this in to the rice it will seem very wet. Keep stirring and the rice will dry as it cools.

MANGO SALSA

Servings: 8 - Prep: 15m - Cooks: 30m - Total: 45m - Additional: 30m

NUTRITION FACTS

Calories: 21, Carbohydrates: 5.4g, Fat: 0.1g, Protein: 0.3g, Cholesterol: 0mg

INGREDIENTS

- 1 mango - peeled, seeded, and chopped
- 1 fresh jalapeno chile pepper, finely chopped
- 1/4 cup finely chopped red bell pepper
- 2 tablespoons lime juice
- 1 green onion, chopped
- 1 tablespoon lemon juice
- 2 tablespoons chopped cilantro

DIRECTIONS

1. In a medium bowl, mix mango, red bell pepper, green onion, cilantro, jalapeno, lime juice, and lemon juice. Cover, and allow to sit at least 30 minutes before serving.

MOROCCAN-STYLE STUFFED ACORN SQUASH

Servings: 4 - Prep: 15m - Cooks: 45m - Total: 1h

NUTRITION FACTS

Calories: 502, Carbohydrates: 93.8g, Fat: 11.7g, Protein: 11.2g, Cholesterol: 10mg

INGREDIENTS

- 2 tablespoons brown sugar
- 1 cup garbanzo beans, drained
- 1 tablespoon butter, melted
- ½ cup raisins
- 2 large acorn squash, halved and seeded
- 1 ½ tablespoons ground cumin
- 2 tablespoons olive oil
- salt and pepper to taste
- 2 cloves garlic, chopped

- 1 (14 ounce) can chicken broth
- 2 stalks celery, chopped
- 1 cup uncooked couscous
- 2 carrots, chopped

DIRECTIONS

1. Preheat oven to 350 degrees F (175 degrees C).
2. Arrange squash halves cut side down on a baking sheet. Bake 30 minutes, or until tender. Dissolve the sugar in the melted butter. Brush squash with the butter mixture, and keep squash warm while preparing the stuffing.
3. Heat the olive oil in a skillet over medium heat. Stir in the garlic, celery, and carrots, and cook 5 minutes. Mix in the garbanzo beans and raisins. Season with cumin, salt, and pepper, and continue to cook and stir until vegetables are tender.
4. Pour the chicken broth into the skillet, and mix in the couscous. Cover skillet, and turn off heat. Allow couscous to absorb liquid for 5 minutes. Stuff squash halves with the skillet mixture to serve.

SLOW COOKER HONEY GARLIC CHICKEN

Servings: 10 - Prep: 20m - Cooks: 4h - Total: 4h20m

NUTRITION FACTS

Calories: 235, Carbohydrates: 34.4g, Fat: 6g, Protein: 13g, Cholesterol: 42mg

INGREDIENTS

- 1 tablespoon vegetable oil
- 2 cloves garlic, crushed
- 10 boneless, skinless chicken thighs
- 1 tablespoon minced fresh ginger root
- 3/4 cup honey
- 1 (20 ounce) can pineapple tidbits, drained with juice reserved
- 3/4 cup lite soy sauce
- 2 tablespoons cornstarch
- 3 tablespoons ketchup
- 1/4 cup water

DIRECTIONS

1. Heat oil in a skillet over medium heat, and cook chicken thighs just until evenly browned on all sides. Place thighs in a slow cooker.
2. In a bowl, mix honey, soy sauce, ketchup, garlic, ginger, and reserved pineapple juice. Pour into the slow cooker.
3. Cover, and cook 4 hours on High. Stir in pineapple tidbits just before serving.

4. mix the cornstarch and water in a small bowl. remove thighs from slow cooker. blend the cornstarch mixture into remaining sauce in the slow cooker to thicken. serve sauce over the chicken.

TASTY LENTIL TACOS

Servings: 6 - Prep: 10m - Cooks: 40m - Total: 50m

NUTRITION FACTS

Calories: 304, Carbohydrates: 44.2g, Fat: 10g, Protein: 9.4g, Cholesterol: 1mg

INGREDIENTS

- 1 teaspoon canola oil
- 1 tablespoon taco seasoning, or to taste
- 2/3 cup finely chopped onion
- 1 2/3 cups chicken broth
- 1 small clove garlic, minced
- 2/3 cup salsa
- 2/3 cup dried lentils, rinsed
- 12 taco shells

DIRECTIONS

1. Heat oil in a skillet over medium heat; cook and stir onion and garlic until tender, about 5 minutes. Mix lentils and taco seasoning into onion mixture; cook and stir for 1 minute.
2. Pour chicken broth into skillet and bring to a boil. Reduce heat to low, cover the skillet, and simmer until lentils are tender, 25 to 30 minutes.
3. Uncover the skillet and cook until mixture is slightly thickened, 6 to 8 minutes. Mash lentils slightly; stir in salsa.
4. Serve about 1/4 cup lentil mixture in each taco shell.

VEGGIE BURGERS

Servings: 8 - Prep: 15m - Cooks: 20m - Total: 1h35m

NUTRITION FACTS

Calories: 193, Carbohydrates: 31.9g, Fat: 4.3g, Protein: 6.9g, Cholesterol: 27mg

INGREDIENTS

- 2 teaspoons olive oil
- 1 ½ cups rolled oats
- 1 small onion, grated
- 1/4 cup shredded Cheddar cheese

- 2 cloves crushed garlic
- 1 egg, beaten
- 2 carrots, shredded
- 1 tablespoon soy sauce
- 1 small summer squash, shredded
- 1 ½ cups all-purpose flour
- 1 small zucchini, shredded

DIRECTIONS

1. Heat the olive oil in a skillet over low heat, and cook the onion and garlic for about 5 minutes, until tender. Mix in the carrots, squash, and zucchini. Continue to cook and stir for 2 minutes. Remove pan from heat, and mix in oats, cheese, and egg. Stir in soy sauce, transfer the mixture to a bowl, and refrigerate 1 hour.

2. Preheat the grill for high heat.

3. Place the flour on a large plate. Form the vegetable mixture into eight 3 inch round patties. Drop each patty into the flour, lightly coating both sides.

4. Oil the grill grate, and grill patties 5 minutes on each side, or until heated through and nicely browned.

RED PEPPER & BEAN TIKKA MASALA

Prep:10 mins **Cook:**20 mins

Serves 2

INGREDIENTS

- 1 tbsp vegetable oil

1 onion, chopped

2 red peppers, deseeded and cut into strips

1 garlic clove, crushed

thumb-sized piece of ginger, grated

1 red chilli, finely chopped

- ½ tbsp garam masala
- ½ tbsp curry powder
- 1 tbsp tomato purée
- 415g can baked beans

½ lemon, juiced

- rice and coriander, to serve

METHOD

STEP 1

Heat the oil in a saucepan over a medium heat, add the onion and red peppers with a pinch of salt and fry until softened, around 5 mins. Tip in the garlic, ginger and red chilli along with the spices and fry for a couple of mins longer.

STEP 2

Spoon in the tomato purée, stir, then tip in the baked beans along with 100ml water. Bubble for 5 mins, then squeeze in the lemon juice. Serve with the rice and scatter over the coriander leaves.

BASIC CURRIED ROAST CHICKPEAS

Prep:5 mins **Cook:**20 mins

Serves 4

INGREDIENTS

- 2 x 400g cans chickpeas
- 1½ tbsp rapeseed oil
- 1 tsp caraway seeds
- 1 tsp mustard seeds
- 1 tbsp curry powder

METHOD

STEP 1

Heat oven to 200C/180C fan/gas 6. Drain the chickpeas and pat with a tea towel to remove as much moisture as possible. Tip them onto a roasting tray, toss with the oil, seeds and seasoning and roast for 20 mins until golden brown. Toss in the curry powder and enjoy.

LENTIL & CAULIFLOWER CURRY

Prep:10 mins **Cook:**40 mins

Serves 4

INGREDIENTS

- 1 tbsp olive oil
- 1 large onion, chopped
- 3 tbsp curry paste
- 1 tsp turmeric
- 1 tsp mustard seeds
- 200g red or yellow lentil
- 1l low-sodium vegetable or chicken stock (made with 2 cubes)
- 1 large cauliflower, broken into florets
- 1 large potato, diced
- 3 tbsp coconut yogurt
- small pack coriander, chopped
- juice 1 lemon
- 100g cooked brown rice

METHOD

STEP 1

Heat the oil in a large saucepan and cook the onion until soft, about 5 mins. Add the curry paste, spices and lentils, then stir to coat the lentils in the onions and paste. Pour over the stock and simmer for 20 mins, then add the cauliflower, potato and a little extra water if it looks a bit dry.

STEP 2

Simmer for about 12 mins until the cauliflower and potatoes are tender. Stir in the yogurt, coriander and lemon juice, and serve with the brown rice.

SPICY CHICKEN & BEAN STEW

Prep:15 mins **Cook:**1 hr and 20 mins

Serves 6

INGREDIENTS

- 1¼ kg chicken thighs and drumsticks (approx. weight, we used a 1.23kg mixed pack)
- 1 tbsp olive oil
- 2 onions, sliced
- 1 garlic clove, crushed
- 2 red chillies, deseeded and chopped
- 250g frozen peppers, defrosted
- 400g can chopped tomatoes
- 420g can kidney beans in chilli sauce
- 2 x 400g cans butter beans, drained
- 400ml hot chicken stock
- small bunch coriander, chopped
- 150ml pot soured cream and crusty bread, to serve

METHOD

STEP 1

Pull the skin off the chicken and discard. Heat the oil in a large casserole dish, brown the chicken all over, then remove with a slotted spoon. Tip in the onions, garlic and chillies, then fry for 5 mins until starting to soften and turn golden.

STEP 2

Add the peppers, tomatoes, beans and hot stock. Put the chicken back on top, half-cover with a pan lid and cook for 50 mins, until the chicken is cooked through and tender.

STEP 3

Stir through the coriander and serve with soured cream and crusty bread.

ORANGE & RASPBERRY GRANOLA

Prep:15 mins **Cook:**25 mins plus at least 1 hr chilling

Serves 4

INGREDIENTS

- 400g jumbo oats
- juice 2 oranges (150ml), plus zest of 1/2

- 1 tsp ground cinnamon
- 2 tbsp freeze-dried raspberries or strawberries (see tip)

25g flaked almonds, toasted

- 25g mixed seeds (such as sunflower, pumpkin, sesame and linseed)

To serve

2 large oranges, peeled and segmented

- mint leaves (optional)

METHOD

STEP 1

Put 200g oats and 500ml water in a food processor and blitz for 1 min. Line a sieve with clean muslin and pour in the oat mixture. Leave to drip through for 5 mins, then twist the ends of the muslin and squeeze well to capture as much of the oat milk as possible – it should be the consistency of single cream. Best chilled at least 1 hr before serving. Can be kept in a sealed or covered jug in the fridge for up to 3 days.

STEP 2

Heat oven to 200C/180C fan/gas 6 and line a baking tray with baking parchment. Put the orange juice in a medium saucepan and bring to the boil. Boil rapidly for 5 mins or until the liquid has reduced by half, stirring occasionally. Mix the remaining 200g oats with the orange zest and cinnamon. Remove the pan from the heat and stir the oat mixture into the juice. Spread over the lined tray in a thin layer and bake for 10-15 mins or until lightly browned and crisp, turning the oats every few mins. Leave to cool on the tray.

STEP 3

Once cool, mix the oats with the raspberries, flaked almonds and seeds. Can be kept in a sealed jar for up to one week. To serve, spoon the granola into bowls, pour over the oat milk and top with the orange segments and mint leaves, if you like.

HERBY CHICKEN GYROS

Prep:10 mins **Cook:**4 mins

Serves 2

INGREDIENTS

- 1 large skinless chicken breast

rapeseed oil, for brushing

small garlic clove, crushed

- ½ tsp dried oregano
- 2 tbsp Greek yogurt

10 cm piece cucumber, grated, excess juice squeezed out

2 tbsp chopped mint, plus a few leaves to serve

- 2 wholemeal pitta breads

2 red or yellow tomatoes, sliced

- 1 red pepper from a jar (not in oil), deseeded and sliced

METHOD

STEP 1

Cut the chicken breast in half lengthways, then cover with cling film and bash with a rolling pin to flatten it. Brush with some oil, then cover with the garlic, oregano and some pepper. Heat a non-stick frying pan and cook the chicken for a few mins each side. Meanwhile, mix the yogurt, cucumber and mint to make tzatziki.

STEP 2

Cut the tops from the pittas along their longest side and stuff with the chicken, tomato, pepper and tzatziki. Poke in a few mint leaves to serve. If taking to the office for lunch, pack the tzatziki in a separate pot and add just before eating to prevent the pitta going soggy before lunchtime.

ROAST ROOTS WITH GOAT'S CHEESE & SPINACH

Prep:30 mins **Cook:**55 mins

Serves 2

INGREDIENTS

350g butternut squash, deseeded and cut into chunks, peeled if you like

200g carrots, peeled and cut into long batons

250g parsnips, peeled and cut into long batons

200g raw beetroot, well-scrubbed and cut into thick wedges

1 medium red onion, cut into wedges

* 1 tbsp cold-pressed rapeseed oil
* juice and finely grated zest 1 lemon

1 bulb garlic, cloves separated

4-5 thyme sprigs, leaves roughly chopped

* 75g soft rindless goat's cheese log

25g mixed nuts, such as brazils, almonds, hazelnuts, pecans and walnuts, roughly chopped

* 50g baby leaf spinach

METHOD

STEP 1

Heat oven to 200C/180C fan/gas 6. Put the vegetables, without the garlic, into a bowl and toss with the oil, lemon zest and juice and plenty of ground black pepper.

STEP 2

Scatter the vegetables over a large baking tray or roasting tin and bake for 30 mins. Take the tray out of the oven, add the garlic and thyme, then turn the vegetables. Return to the oven for 20 mins or until the vegetables are tender and lightly browned, turning halfway through. Dot with the goat's cheese and nuts, scatter over the spinach and return to the oven for 3-5 mins or until the spinach has wilted and the goat's cheese has begun to melt. You can press the softened garlic cloves out of their skins and mash with the roasted vegetables, if you like.

SPICE-CRUSTED AUBERGINES & PEPPERS WITH PILAF

Prep:10 mins **Cook:**30 mins

Serves 4

INGREDIENTS

2 large aubergines, halved

* 2 tbsp extra virgin olive oil

2 red peppers, quartered

* 2 tsp ground cinnamon
* 2 tsp chilli flakes
* 2 tsp za'atar
* 4 tbsp pomegranate molasses
* 140g puy lentils
* 140g basmati rice
* seeds from 1 pomegranate

small pack flat-leaf parsley, roughly chopped

Greek or coconut yogurt, to serve

METHOD

STEP 1

Heat oven to 220C/200C fan/gas 7. Using a sharp knife, score a diamond pattern into the aubergines. Brush with 1 tbsp of the oil, season well and place on a baking tray, cut-side down. Cook in the oven for 15 mins. Add the peppers to the tray, turn the aubergines over and drizzle everything with the remaining oil. Sprinkle over the spices, 1 tbsp of the pomegranate molasses and a little salt. Roast in the oven for 15 mins more.

STEP 2

Boil the lentils in plenty of water until al dente. After they've been boiling for 5 mins, add the rice. Cook for 10 mins or until cooked through but with a bit of bite. Drain and return to the pan, covered with a lid to keep warm.

STEP 3

Stir the pomegranate seeds and parsley through the lentil rice. Divide between four plates or tip onto a large platter. Top with the roasted veg, a dollop of yogurt and the remaining pomegranate molasses drizzled over.

POTATO PANCAKES WITH CHARD & EGGS

Prep:10 mins **Cook:**15 mins

Serves 2

INGREDIENTS

- 300g mashed potato

4 spring onions, very finely chopped

- 25g plain wholemeal flour
- ½ tsp baking powder
- 3 eggs
- 2 tsp rapeseed oil

240g chard, stalks and leaves roughly chopped, or baby spinach, chopped

METHOD

STEP 1

Mix the mash, spring onions, flour, baking powder and 1 of the eggs in a bowl. Heat the oil in a non-stick frying pan, then spoon in the potato mix to make two mounds. Flatten them to form two 15cm discs and fry for 5-8 mins until the undersides are set and golden, then carefully ip over and cook on the other side.

STEP 2

Meanwhile, wash the chard and put in a pan with some of the water still clinging to it, then cover and cook over a medium heat for 5 mins until wilted and tender. Poach the remaining eggs.

STEP 3

Top the pancakes with the greens and egg. Serve while the yolks are still runny.

BEST POTATOES YOU'LL EVER TASTE

Servings: 4 - Prep: 10m - Cooks: 20m - Total: 30m

NUTRITION FACTS

Calories: 283, Carbohydrates: 47.6g, Fat: 8.5g, Protein: 5.6g, Cholesterol: 4mg

INGREDIENTS

- 3 tablespoons mayonnaise
- salt and pepper to taste
- 2 cloves garlic, crushed
- 5 potatoes, quartered
- 1 teaspoon dried oregano

DIRECTIONS

In a small bowl, mix mayonnaise, garlic, oregano, salt, and pepper. Set aside.

1. Bring a large pot of salted water to a boil. Add potatoes, and cook until almost done, about 10 minutes. Don't overcook otherwise the potatoes will break apart. Drain, and cool.
2. Preheat oven broiler. Line a baking tray with aluminum foil, and lightly grease the aluminum foil.
3. Arrange potatoes in the prepared baking tray. Spoon the mayonnaise mixture over the potatoes. Place on the prepared grill, and cook until potatoes are tender and mayonnaise mixture is lightly browned, about 10 minutes.

VEGETARIAN MEATLOAF WITH VEGETABLES

Servings: 9 - Prep: 20m - Cooks: 1h30m - Total: 1h50m

NUTRITION FACTS

Calories: 225, Carbohydrates: 30.6g, Fat: 4.9g, Protein: 15.1g, Cholesterol: 42mg

INGREDIENTS

- ½ (14 ounce) package vegetarian ground beef (e.g., Gimme Lean TM)
- 2 teaspoons prepared mustard
- 1 (12 ounce) package vegetarian burger crumbles
- 1 tablespoon vegetable oil
- 1 onion, chopped
- 3 ½ slices bread, cubed
- 2 eggs, beaten
- 1/3 cup milk
- 2 tablespoons vegetarian Worcestershire sauce
- 1 (8 ounce) can tomato sauce
- 1 teaspoon salt
- 4 carrots, cut into 1 inch pieces
- 1/3 teaspoon pepper
- 4 potatoes, cubed
- 1 teaspoon ground sage
- 1 cooking spray

- ½ teaspoon garlic powder

DIRECTIONS

1. Preheat oven to 350 degrees F (175 degrees C).
2. In a large bowl combine vegetarian ground beef, vegetarian ground beef crumbles, onion, eggs, Worcestershire sauce, salt, pepper, sage, garlic powder, mustard, oil, bread cubes and milk. Transfer to a 9 x 13 inch baking dish and form into a loaf. Pour tomato sauce on top.
3. Place carrots and potatoes around loaf and spray vegetables with cooking spray.
4. Bake 30 to 45 minutes; turn vegetables. Bake another 30 to 45 minutes. Let stand 15 minutes before slicing.

BRUSSELS SPROUTS IN MUSTARD SAUCE

Servings: 6 - Prep: 10m - Cooks: 20m - Total: 30m

NUTRITION FACTS

Calories: 41, Carbohydrates: 9.4g, Fat: 0.4g, Protein: 1.9g, Cholesterol: 0mg

INGREDIENTS

- 2 tablespoons cornstarch
- 1 pound Brussels sprouts
- 1/4 cup water
- 2 teaspoons prepared Dijon-style mustard
- 1 (14.5 ounce) can chicken broth
- 2 teaspoons lemon juice

DIRECTIONS

1. Dissolve cornstarch in 1/4 cup water, and set aside.
2. In a medium saucepan over medium heat, bring chicken broth to a boil. Add Brussels sprouts, and cook until tender. Strain, reserving chicken broth, and place Brussels sprouts in a warm serving dish.
3. Return chicken broth to stove, stir in mustard and lemon juice, and return to boil. Add cornstarch mixture. Cook and stir until thickened. Pour over Brussels sprouts to serve.

ORZO WITH KALE

Servings: 10 - Prep: 10m - Cooks: 25m - Total: 35m

NUTRITION FACTS

Calories: 206, Carbohydrates: 36.1g, Fat: 4.2g, Protein: 7.9g, Cholesterol: 2mg

INGREDIENTS

- 1 teaspoon ground turmeric
- 1 large lemon, juiced
- 2 cups uncooked orzo pasta
- 1/4 teaspoon ground nutmeg

- 2 tablespoons olive oil
- 1/4 cup grated Parmesan cheese, or to taste
- 4 cloves garlic, sliced
- salt and black pepper to taste
- 1 bunch kale, stems removed and leaves coarsely chopped

DIRECTIONS

1. Bring a large pot of lightly-salted water to a boil; sprinkle the turmeric over the boiling water and stir in the orzo; return to a boil. Cook uncovered, stirring occasionally, until the pasta has cooked through, but is still firm to the bite, about 11 minutes; drain. Scrape into a mixing bowl and set aside.
2. Heat the olive oil in a large skillet over medium heat. Cook the garlic in the hot oil for a few seconds until it begins to bubble. Stir the kale into the garlic, cover the skillet with a lid, and cook for 10 minutes. Remove the cover and continue cooking and stirring until the kale is tender, about 10 minutes more. Stir the kale mixture into the orzo along with the lemon juice, nutmeg, and Parmesan cheese. Season with salt and pepper. Serve warm or at room temperature.

LEMON PEPPER PASTA

Servings: 8 - Prep: 5m - Cooks: 15m - Total: 20m

NUTRITION FACTS

Calories: 243, Carbohydrates: 43g, Fat: 4.2g, Protein: 7.5g, Cholesterol: 0mg

INGREDIENTS

- 1 pound spaghetti
- 1 tablespoon dried basil
- 2 tablespoons olive oil
- ground black pepper to taste
- 3 tablespoons lemon juice, to taste

DIRECTIONS

1. Bring a large pot of lightly salted water to a boil. Add pasta and cook for 8 to 10 minutes, or until done; drain.
2. In a small bowl, combine olive oil, lemon juice, basil and black pepper. Mix well and toss with the pasta. Serve hot or cold.

PORK CHOP AND CABBAGE CASSEROLE

Servings: 4 - Prep: 30m - Cooks: 1h30m - Total: 2h

NUTRITION FACTS

Calories: 370, Carbohydrates: 54.2g, Fat: 8.3g, Protein: 21.5g, Cholesterol: 42mg

INGREDIENTS

- 1 small head cabbage, shredded

- ½ (10.75 ounce) can water
- 4 potatoes, peeled and sliced
- 1 small onion, diced
- salt to taste
- 4 pork chops
- 1 (10.75 ounce) can condensed cream of chicken soup

DIRECTIONS

1. Preheat oven to 350 degrees F (175 degrees C). Lightly grease a 9x13 baking dish.
2. Place a layer of shredded cabbage into baking dish and then a layer of sliced potatoes. Repeat cabbage and potatoes and salt.
3. Simmer the soup, water and diced onion. Pour over cabbage and potatoes.
4. In a skillet, brown each pork chop in a small amount of oil and place on top of mixture. Bake for 1 ½ hours uncovered or until chops are tender.

COCONUT CRÊPES WITH RASPBERRY SAUCE

Prep:10 mins **Cook:**25 mins

Serves 6

INGREDIENTS

For the raspberry sauce

- 200g raspberries
- 2 tsp cornflour
- 2 tsp maple syrup

For the coconut crêpes

- 140g plain flour
- 2 large eggs
- 300ml coconut milk
- 2 tbsp toasted desiccated coconut

a little sunflower oil, for frying

METHOD

STEP 1

Set aside 6 of the raspberries. Mix the cornflour with 1 tbsp water until smooth. Measure 300ml water in a pan, and stir in the cornflour paste. Heat, stirring, until thickened. Add the remaining raspberries and cook gently, mashing the berries to a pulp. Strain the mixture through a sieve into a bowl to remove the seeds, pushing through as much of the mixture as you can. Quarter the reserved raspberries and add to the sauce, along with the maple syrup.

STEP 2

To make the crêpes, tip the flour and a pinch of salt into a large jug, then beat in the eggs, coconut milk, 200ml water and 11/2 tbsp toasted coconut to make a batter the consistency of double cream. Thin with a little more water if it is too thick. Heat a small frying pan with a dash of oil, then pour in a little batter, swirling the pan so that it completely covers the base. Leave to set over the heat for 1 min, then carefully flip it over and cook the other side for a few secs more. Transfer to a plate and repeat with the remaining batter until you have at least 12. Stir the batter to redistribute the coconut as you use it. Serve 2 crêpes per person with a drizzle of the sauce and a little of the remaining toasted coconut.

LOW-FAT CHERRY CHEESECAKE

Prep:1 hr **Cook:**30 mins Plus overnight chilling

Cuts into 8 slices

INGREDIENTS

25g butter, melted

140g amaretti biscuit, crushed

- 3 sheets leaf gelatine
- zest and juice 1 orange
- 2 x 250g tubs quark
- 250g tub ricotta
- 2 tsp vanilla extract
- 100g icing sugar
- For the topping

400g fresh cherry, stoned

- 5 tbsp cherry jam
- 1 tbsp cornflour

METHOD

STEP 1

Line the sides of a 20cm round loose-bottomed cake tin with baking parchment. Stir the butter into twothirds of the biscuit crumbs, and reserve the rest. Sprinkle the buttery crumbs over the base of the tin and press down. Soak the gelatine in cold water for 5-10 mins until soft.

STEP 2

Warm the orange juice in a small pan or the microwave until almost boiling. Squeeze the gelatine of excess water, then stir into the juice to dissolve.

STEP 3

Beat the quark, ricotta, vanilla and icing sugar together with an electric whisk until really smooth. Then, with the beaters still running, pour in the juice mixture and beat to combine. Pour the cheesecake mixture over the crumbs and smooth the top. Cover with cling film and chill overnight.

STEP 4

To make the topping, put the cherries in a pan with the orange zest and 100ml water. Cook, covered, for 15 mins until the cherries are softened. Put one-third of the cherries in a bowl and mash with a potato masher to give you a chunky compote. Return to the pan, add the jam, cornflour and 2 tbsp water, and mix to combine. Cook until thickened and saucy – if the sauce is too dry, add a splash more water. Cool to room temperature.

STEP 5

Just before serving, carefully remove the cheesecake from the tin and peel off the parchment. Scatter over the remaining biscuit crumbs and some cherry sauce. Serve in slices with the remaining cherry sauce alongside.

JAM TURNOVERS

Prep:10 mins **Cook:**20 mins

Serves 6

INGREDIENTS

- 320g sheet puff pastry
- 1 heaped tbsp jam (apricot, raspberry or strawberry work well)
- 1 beaten egg

icing sugar, for dusting

clotted cream, to serve

METHOD

STEP 1

Heat the oven to 200C/180C fan/gas 6. Unravel the puff pastry on a lightly floured surface. Cut the pastry into six squares. Spoon the jam in the centre of each pastry square. Seal the edges by pressing down with a fork and brush with the egg. Lay on a lined baking sheet and bake for 20 mins. Dust with the icing sugar and serve with the clotted cream.

ROASTED GREEN BEANS

Servings: 4 - Prep: 10m - Cooks: 20m - Total: 30m

NUTRITION FACTS

Calories: 101, Carbohydrates: 16.4g, Fat: 3.7g, Protein: 4.2g, Cholesterol: 0mg

INGREDIENTS

- 2 pounds fresh green beans, trimmed
- 1 teaspoon kosher salt
- 1 tablespoon olive oil, or as needed
- ½ teaspoon freshly ground black pepper

DIRECTIONS

1. Preheat oven to 400 degrees F (200 degrees C).
2. Pat green beans dry with paper towels if necessary; spread onto a jellyroll pan. Drizzle with olive oil and sprinkle with salt and pepper. Use your fingers to coat beans evenly with olive oil and spread them out so they don't overlap.
3. Roast in the preheated oven until beans are slightly shriveled and have brown spots, 20 to 25 minutes.

EGG FRIED RICE

Servings: 4 - Prep: 5m - Cooks: 15m - Total: 20m

NUTRITION FACTS

Calories: 145, Carbohydrates: 24.6g, Fat: 2.7g, Protein: 4.9g, Cholesterol: 46mg

INGREDIENTS

- 1 cup water
- ½ onion, finely chopped
- ½ teaspoon salt
- ½ cup green beans

- 2 tablespoons soy sauce
- 1 egg, lightly beaten
- 1 cup uncooked instant rice
- 1/4 teaspoon ground black pepper
- 1 teaspoon vegetable oil

DIRECTIONS

1. In a saucepan bring water, salt and soy sauce to a boil. Add rice and stir. Remove from heat, cover and let stand 5 minutes.
2. Heat oil in a medium skillet or wok over medium heat. Saute onions and green beans for 2 to 3 minutes. Pour in egg and fry for 2 minutes, scrambling egg while it cooks.
3. Stir in the cooked rice, mix well and sprinkle with pepper.

VEGGIE OKONOMIYAKI

Prep:15 mins **Cook:**10 mins

Serves 2

INGREDIENTS

- 3 large eggs
- 50g plain flour
- 50ml milk

4 spring onions, trimmed and sliced

1 pak choi, sliced

200g Savoy cabbage, shredded

1 red chilli, deseeded and finely chopped, plus extra to serve

- ½ tbsp low-salt soy sauce
- ½ tbsp rapeseed oil
- 1 heaped tbsp low-fat mayonnaise

½ lime, juiced

sushi ginger, to serve (optional)

wasabi, to serve (optional)

METHOD

STEP 1

Whisk together the eggs, flour and milk until smooth. Add half the spring onions, the pak choi, cabbage, chilli and soy sauce. Heat the oil in a small frying pan and pour in the batter. Cook, covered, over a medium heat for 7-8 mins. Flip the okonomiyaki into a second frying pan, then return it to the heat and cook for a further 7-8 mins until a skewer inserted into it comes out clean.

STEP 2

Mix the mayonnaise and lime juice together in a small bowl. Transfer the okonomiyaki to a plate, then drizzle over the lime mayo and top with the extra chilli and spring onion and the sushi ginger, if using. Serve with the wasabi on the side, if you like.

EASY CHICKEN STEW

Prep:10 mins **Cook:**50 mins

Serves 4

INGREDIENTS

- 1 tbsp olive oil

1 bunch spring onions, sliced, white and green parts separated

- 1 small swede (350g), peeled and chopped into small pieces

400g potatoes, peeled and chopped into small pieces

- 8 skinless boneless chicken thighs
- 1 tbsp Dijon mustard
- 500ml chicken stock
- 200g Savoy cabbage or spring cabbage, sliced
- 2 tsp cornflour (optional)
- crusty bread or cheese scones, to serve (optional)

METHOD

STEP 1

Heat the oil in a large saucepan. Add the white spring onion slices and fry for 1 min to soften. Tip in the swede and potatoes and cook for 2-3 mins more, then add the chicken, mustard and stock. Cover and cook for 35 mins, or until the vegetables are tender and the chicken cooked through.

STEP 2

Add the cabbage and simmer for another 5 mins. If the stew looks too thin, mix the cornflour with 1 tbsp cold water and pour a couple of teaspoonfuls into the pan; let the stew bubble and thicken, then check again. If it's still too thin, add a little more of the cornflour mix and let the stew bubble and thicken some more.

STEP 3

Season to taste, then spoon the stew into deep bowls. Scatter over the green spring onion slices and serve with crusty bread or warm cheese scones, if you like.

LAST-MINUTE CHRISTMAS LOAF CAKE

Prep:25 mins **Cook:**1 hr and 15 mins Plus 2 hrs soaking

Serves 10

INGREDIENTS

- 200g raisins and sultanas
- 50g sour cherries

100g dried figs, chopped

- 150g mixed peel

1 orange, zested and juiced

- 250ml brandy

115g butter, plus extra melted for the tin

- 115g muscovado sugar

4 eggs, beaten

- 120g self-raising flour
- 1 tsp baking powder
- 60g brioche crumbs
- 40g chopped pecans and pistachios

- ½ tsp ground mace
- ½ tsp ground cinnamon

icing sugar, to serve (optional)

METHOD

STEP 1

Tip the fruit and peel into a bowl with the orange juice and zest and 150ml of the brandy. Stir well, then leave in a warm place for 2 hrs for the fruit to plump up.

STEP 2

Heat oven to 170C/150C fan/gas 4. Brush a 900g loaf tin with the melted butter, then line with baking parchment. Beat the muscovado sugar and butter until light and fluffy, then add the eggs one at a time. Mix in the fruit and the rest of the ingredients except for the remaining brandy and icing sugar. Spoon the mixture into the loaf tin, put the tin in a deep tray and bake for 1 hr 15 mins-1 hr 30 mins or until a skewer prodded in comes out clean. Remove from the oven and immediately pour over the brandy (this makes it easier for the cake to soak it up). Leave to cool, then dust with icing sugar, if using.

GREEN CHOWDER WITH PRAWNS

Prep:10 mins **Cook:**20 mins - 30 mins

Serves 4

INGREDIENTS

- 1 tbsp olive oil

1 onion, finely chopped

1 celery stick, finely chopped

- 1 garlic clove
- 300g petit pois
- 200g pack sliced kale

2 potatoes, finely chopped

- 1 low-salt chicken stock cube (we used Kallo)
- 100g cooked North Atlantic prawns

METHOD

STEP 1

Heat the oil in a saucepan over a medium heat. Add the onion and celery and cook for 5-6 mins until softened but not coloured. Add the garlic and cook for a further min. Stir in the petit pois, kale and potatoes, then add the stock cube and 750ml water. Bring to the boil and simmer for 10-12 mins until the potatoes are soft.

STEP 2

Tip ¾ of the mixture into a food processor and whizz until smooth. Add a little more water or stock if it's too thick. Pour the mixture back into the pan and add half the prawns.

STEP 3

Divide between four bowls and spoon the remaining prawns on top. Can be frozen for up to a month. Add the prawns once defrosted.

MUSHROOM BRUNCH

Prep:5 mins **Cook:**12 mins - 15 mins

Serves 4

INGREDIENTS

- 250g mushrooms
- 1 garlic clove
- 1 tbsp olive oil
- 160g bag kale
- 4 eggs

METHOD

STEP 1

Slice the mushrooms and crush the garlic clove. Heat the olive oil in a large non-stick frying pan, then fry the garlic over a low heat for 1 min. Add the mushrooms and cook until soft. Then, add the kale. If the kale won't all fit in the pan, add half and stir until wilted, then add the rest. Once all the kale is wilted, season.

STEP 2

Now crack in the eggs and keep them cooking gently for 2-3 mins. Then, cover with the lid to for a further 2-3 mins or until the eggs are cooked to your liking. Serve with bread.

CAIPIROSKA

Prep:5 mins **Serves 1**

INGREDIENTS

- 1 lime
- 2 tsp golden granulated sugar
- 50ml vodka
- crushed ice

METHOD

STEP 1

Cut the lime into small chunks, then put it into the bottom of a sturdy tumbler and add the golden granulated sugar. Crush really well with a muddler – you can also do this with a pestle and mortar.

STEP 2

Top up the tumbler with crushed ice, then add the vodka. Stir well to mix all the ingredients together, and servex

SAUSAGE & BUTTERNUT SQUASH SHELLS

Prep:15 mins **Cook:**35 mins

Serves 4

INGREDIENTS

1 medium butternut squash, peeled and cut into medium chunks

- 1 ½ tbsp olive oil

2 garlic cloves, crushed

1 fennel bulb, thinly sliced (keep the green fronds to serve)

4 spring onions, thinly sliced

- 2 tsp chilli flakes
- 1 tsp fennel seeds
- 300g large pasta shells
- 3 pork sausages

METHOD

STEP 1

Put the squash in a microwaveable bowl with a splash of water. Cover with cling film and cook on high for 10 mins until soft. Tip into a blender.

STEP 2

Meanwhile, put a frying pan over a medium heat and pour in 1 tbsp olive oil. Add the garlic, sliced fennel, spring onions, half the chilli flakes, half the fennel seeds and a splash of water. Cook, stirring occasionally, for 5 mins until softened. Scrape into the blender with squash. Blitz to a smooth sauce, adding enough water to get to a creamy consistency. Season to taste.

STEP 3

Bring a pan of water to the boil and cook the pasta for 1 min less than the pack instructions. Put the frying pan back on the heat (don't bother washing it first – it's all flavour). Pour in the remaining oil, squeeze the sausagemeat from the skins into the pan and add the remaining chilli and remaining fennel seeds. Fry until browned and crisp, breaking down the sausagemeat with a spoon.

STEP 4

Drain the pasta and return to its pan on the heat. Pour in the butternut sauce and give everything a good mix to warm the sauce through. Divide between bowls and top with the crispy sausage mix and fennel fronds.

www.ingramcontent.com/pod-product-compliance
Lightning Source LLC
Chambersburg PA
CBHW080909160726
48000CB00009B/2920